Tree of Knowledge, Tree of Life

RICHARD CHARTRES

D1359737

MOREHOUSE PUBLISHING
A Continuum imprint
www.morehousepublishing.com

Morehouse
4775 Linglestow Road
Harrisburg
PA 17112

Continuum
The Tower Building
11 York Road
London SE1 7NX

Morehouse is an imprint of Continuum Books

www.continuumbooks.com

First published 2005

British Library Cataloguing-in-Publication Data
A catalogue record for this book is available from the British Library.

ISBN 0 8192 8123 9

Choruses from The Rock, from *Collected Poems 1909–1962* by
T. S. Eliot, published by Faber and Faber Ltd.
'Robert Runcie' reproduced with kind permission. Previously
published in *Runcie, On Reflection*, edited by Stephen Platten,
Canterbury Press.

Typeset by Kenneth Burnley, Wirral, Cheshire
Printed and bound by Cromwell Press, Trowbridge, Wiltshire

Contents

Contents

Part 3: On Various Occasions

Foreword and
Acknowledgements

No modern Bishop of London can pretend to be an original scholar. Even Mandell Creighton, the historian of the Papacy, acknowledged that his contribution to scholarship ceased with his appointment to the See of London. That was in the closing years of Queen Victoria's reign, and so it has been ever since.

There are contemporary privileges, however. Being Bishop of London and Dean of Chapels Royal offers the incumbent a modest role in public ceremonial and an introduction to some of the most significant minds and personalities of the day. At the same time the bishop of the capital city (or at least part of it) is constantly challenged by frequent anniversaries and special occasions on which it falls to his lot to attempt some interpretation. It is this experience which is reflected in the following pages.

It should be noted that these scripts were meant to be delivered and heard, and were not destined for the printed page. I am grateful to an old friend, Robin Baird-Smith of Continuum, who cast a dispassionate eye over the filing cabinets full of my more recent effusions and suggested that the following pieces might have some wider interest. Perhaps they will be a little more comprehensible if they are read aloud.

It will be obvious in what follows that I have drawn heavily on the work of many friends, living and departed. My particular thanks go to Margaret Barker, whose conversation and whose book, *The Great High Priest*, have been especially illuminating. That said, I would not have survived a single one of these London years without the love and critical solidarity of the family: Caroline, my wife, Alexander, Sophie, Louis and Clio.

Richard Chartres

Part 1

TREE OF KNOWLEDGE, TREE OF LIFE

1

Tree of Knowledge, Tree of Life

The fear of the Lord is the beginning of wisdom:
a good understanding have all they that do here-
after; the praise of it endureth for ever. (Psalm
111.10)

I wish to reflect with you on the relationship between
wisdom, knowledge and information, with particular
reference to our life together as Christians in today's
world.

T. S. Eliot, churchwarden in the Diocese of London,
thought that there was a problem. As he said in one of
the choruses from *The Rock* (1934):

Where is the wisdom we have lost in knowledge?
Where is the knowledge we have lost in information?

This is of course an ancient question. In the myth of
the Paradise Garden we are presented with two trees:
the Tree of Life and the Tree of Knowledge. The fruit of
the Tree of Life was true knowledge of the divine
creation. This is what the biblical tradition regards

as wisdom. 'Wisdom is a tree of life to them that lay hold upon her' (Proverbs 3.18).

What of the Tree of Knowledge? This is knowledge wrenched from its source which, according to the first book of Enoch, 'caused much bloodshed on the earth'. The knowledge from the second tree is partial and fragmented. It is knowledge only of a God-forsaken world in which human beings themselves have assumed the role of gods. In the process of course they have discovered that, abstracted from the creator and source of life, their destiny is death.

Wisdom is a way of being in the world, aware of the deep structure of life, respectful of other beings, taking life, not for granted, but with thanksgiving to its Author.

With such awareness it is possible to put knowledge in its proper context and apply it to beneficent ends. This transforming awareness is symbolized in the Bible by anointing. Christ is the anointed one (*Christos* in Greek means 'anointed') who possesses the fullness of the wisdom of God and who is in the world to open up the way to Paradise regained. But, as St Paul declares, this is strange wisdom, which involves self-giving and the embrace of suffering and death as a way to life in all its fullness.

Recent events have caused me to reflect urgently on the way we live now. Last Monday, former Senator Sam Nunn, now head of an agency devoted to mitigating the threat of nuclear, chemical and biological terrorism, gave a speech detailing how easy access to lethal knowledge, derived from the discoveries of the twentieth century, has handed huge potential destructive power to extreme individuals. One of the

4

consequences will obviously be a massive increase in minute surveillance of all our lives; and of course the knowledge to do that already exists.

The message is amplified in one of this year's most important books. Martin Rees, the Astronomer Royal, in his book *Our Final Century* considers whether the human race will survive the twenty-first century. With sobriety and clarity he describes our vulnerable and fragile world and the reality of the dangers we face from not only deranged individuals possessed of lethal knowledge but also from environmental degradation.

Our generation seems to be characterized by a way of relating to the cosmos that is frankly autistic. There is a certain lack of awareness or recognition, which causes us to waste the beauty of the world. There is also technical knowledge, which enables us to have an unparalleled impact as we exploit the earth.

The modern project of growth without limits and with no end in view beyond the process itself, arises, in the perspective of the Abrahamic religions, from choosing the wrong tree. We have lost the knowledge of wisdom in the pursuit of fragmented knowledge.

The pursuit of fragmented knowledge divorced from any consciousness of ourselves as creatures, fashions an individual knower who looks out on the world around and experiences not an animated nature in which he or she is a participant, but simply matter to be exploited. Choosing the wrong tree progressively degrades a human being into someone who gets used to the dull pain of seeing nature as a lifeless desert and of treating its beauty as a deceptive mask. Dominance is substituted for connectedness in this way of knowing the universe. It is a way of knowledge which leads, as Descartes frankly affirmed, to a way of being in the world in which humans regards themselves as 'maître et possesseur de la terre'.

Now, however, things are even more serious. The habit of regarding everything as a material or mental object has even infected our good opinion of ourselves. Beneath much of the rhetoric about human dignity lurks fear and a reductionist suspicion that we are little more than upright animals or, even worse, rapacious bipeds with a selfish genetic make-up, whose happiness lies in consuming the world and treating other people as commodities which exist for our pleasure.

There is another important book recently published which looks at questions of human identity. In *Tomorrow's People*, Susan Greenfield, from a profound scientific base but with a great clarity of expression, explores how twenty-first-century technology is changing the way we feel and think. She contemplates the implications of combining (in ways that are already conceivable) carbon-based and silicon-based life forms like ourselves. I met a charming example the other day, my first 'bionic bishop'. This most spiritual and delightful retired man has received a minute eye implant using nano-technology, which has restored his sight to what it was in his twenties. I am certainly not a techno-phobe and rejoice with everyone else at such alleviations of the human lot.

But there must be a real possibility, prefigured in Huxley's *Brave New World*, that the human race, given the unequal distribution of power and wealth, could divide into a rich and powerful élite of gene- and silicon-enriched individuals, supported or even directed by super-intelligent, self-replicating machines, and well defended against the multitudinous rest, the 'naturals'. We have just experienced a 'virtual reality' state visit in which only a very few were permitted to see the President in the flesh while he was able to enjoy the ordinary delights of a pub lunch only as an artfully constructed, security-assured scenario.

Soon it will not be necessary at all to travel to enjoy any scenario you choose. With ample technical means to control our emotions, I imagine that addictions to artificial emotional experiences will be easy to induce and then we shall indeed be 'such stuff as dreams are made on'. Who is to gainsay us these pleasures and this escape from the world we have fashioned? Who is to be our judge? Who is to say that one set of values is better than another set or that any values might be preferred to self-serving hedonism? Before we say that it will never happen, we might reflect on why the government has recently expressed concern about how very young children are relating or failing to relate to one another socially.

Sitting down to discuss these problems is doubtless useful, but since they arise from an atrophying of our human and especially creaturely awareness, mere appeals to ethics and fraternity will not evoke the energy necessary for transformation while we can still see the peril. The risk is that knowledge apart from wisdom will rapidly bring so many changes that, like the frog in the saucepan, we shall be unaware that we are being cooked.

The Christian community will convince and make a contribution to enlarging a healthy human vision, not by mere descriptions, no matter how eloquent, of the state we are in. We shall convince only by a radical and disciplined engagement with Christ as the wisdom of God. This means for us all, if we dare to call ourselves Christians, self-giving to the daily work of prayer which reaches out to the centre of ourselves beyond ourselves, which communicates with the beyond, in silence and stillness. This is hard work, but it is the way of making progress in the kind of research that our contemporaries will find convincing.

Then alongside this kind of de-centring prayer is dedication to seeing and serving the Spirit of Christ in one another and indeed in the lives of those who have no time for Christ. If we are following the wisdom of God this means paying special attention to the poor and seeing them as our teachers. This is of course a way which involves suffering, but the wisdom of God has always been inseparable from suffering and death embraced and not denied. This is the way to joy, to life in all its fullness, to eternal life.

Unless we can exhibit convincing research results, and a glimpse of the human life in community that God intended, then I fear that it will be hard indeed to marshal arguments against the possibility that the future of this world (and perhaps even the judiciary) will lie with intelligent machines rather than human beings.

'Hath not God made foolish the wisdom of the world? . . . But Christ is the power and the wisdom of God' (1 Corinthians 1.19, 24).

Lincoln's Inn
23 November 2003

Part 2

THROUGH THE YEAR

2

Ash Wednesday (1)

'A day of darkness and gloominess', says the prophet (Joel 2.1–2). We experience the clouds in this great world city this Ash Wednesday. There is a cocktail of fear: fear of economic decline, fear of war, fear of the consequences of arming terrorists with the lethal knowledge of poison and disease now so easily and ironically accessible through one of our greatest technical achievements, the Internet.

The fear is concealed of course by a hectic lifestyle which also suppresses a fear of death itself in living faster and faster in the vain hope that we shall get more out of this short life. The fear grows in proportion to our not confronting it. It pushes us to do irrational things, to turn our hatred upon scapegoats.

I wonder what influences the crowd in the Gospel were under, the crowd swirling about the Temple in Jerusalem, that world city occupied by a foreign power, a maelstrom of anxiety then as now? They had fastened upon an unfortunate woman caught in the act of adultery. As we reel from our betrayals and secret cravings, how good to focus on some malefactor caught red-handed. We think of the crowds who scream their hatred at paedophiles. Child abuse, like adultery, is a sin. Let us not be sentimental: it is a terrible thing to use other people for our pleasure as if they were mere objects to be consumed for our gratification. But the extreme anger of the homicidal crowd is fuelled from the shadow world within, where an even darker and deeper game is being played out.

The tempest breaks on Jesus Christ. Come on Jesus, the law says this woman ought to be stoned to death. What does he do? He stoops down and with his finger writes upon the ground. He disengages from the tempest. He bows down and offers a healthy pause.

We are all over-stimulated. Blessed Lent, the sad springtime of the Church's year, is the time when we support each other as believers in simplifying our lives; removing fuel from the fires of rage and fear; facing a little more of the shadow world within by laying aside some of our usual comforters, our anaesthetizers that we use to deaden the pain.

The discipline of Lent in a simpler world used to centre on food. The ancient Christian discipline is salutary for us in a time when there seems to be perpetual carnival and no ensuing Lent, no joyful rhythm of fasting and feasting but insatiate feeding.

The ancient prescription is that Christians observe a total fast on Ash Wednesday and Good Friday. During the rest of Lent the traditional rule is to abstain from meat, dairy products and alcohol and then in the final three weeks to fast during daylight hours on Monday, Wednesday and Friday. Practice was always adapted to personal circumstances.

In our time, however, a break from other forms of overstimulation may be even more appropriate. These are matters which you should discuss with your soul friend; but let us take Lent seriously as an antidote to the indigestion which follows the attempt to live according to the modern recipe of growth without limit, with no end in view beyond the process itself.

After the disengagement, Jesus lifted himself up and saw them with devastating clarity and asked with appalling directness, 'He that is without sin, let him cast the first stone.' Silence and stillness, stooping down to the ground: that is the great education in awareness. Such was the awareness of Jesus Christ that he was able to bring others into his light and up to his level as he lifted himself up. They began to melt away and Jesus was left alone with the victim, who was not allowed to treat herself as a victim; but he gives her responsibility as he says, 'I do not condemn thee, go thy way, sin no more.'

We have faced the fear and the rage and even our tendency to feel sorry for ourselves and to blame others for our misfortunes. Seeing things in the light of Jesus Christ, the human face of God and in the silence and stillness – the woman you notice wisely does not say anything except to answer his question with great simplicity – we are convicted and healed in the same instant by the loving compassion of God who desires for us health and that we should be lifted up to his level.

This is a very mysterious world. We have abundance but we have vast numbers of people in the world who are vulnerable and poor through no fault of their own. This could be a Paradise in 30 seconds if there was a universal change of heart; but instead it is from the heart that the fear and hatreds emerge which expose

us all and our children to the dangers of war. Let us
this Lent make some progress to filling our own empti-
ness with the peaceable spirit of Jesus Christ. Let us
at the very least share a little of what we have with
those who are facing the terrible scourge of AIDS in
Mozambique with whom we, in the Church of London,
are united by a covenant ratified in this very cathedral. This is the way that we enter most profoundly
into the most true mystery that God is 'gracious and
full of compassion, slow to anger and plenteous in
mercy'. And that he intends us to find not gloom or fear
but delight and fulfilment as we live in harmony with
the deep structure of the world he has made.

St Paul's Cathedral
Ash Wednesday 2003

3

Ash Wednesday (2)

O blessed day! At a time when we are tempted to act out perpetual carnival with no ensuing Lent, here is the beginning of the sad but beautiful springtime of the Church's year, inspiring us to rediscover the rhythms which are integral to a spiritually attuned life.

The submerging of the rhythms of the day, the week and the year which connect us to the other parts of the creation, to the sun and the moon and the seasons, by a hectic tide of getting and spending, leaves us dangerously exposed to spiritual exhaustion. Paradoxically, as each moment is hyped in a life which lacks light and shade, feast and fast as part of a coherent pattern embracing the whole year, then everything is reduced to a dull average. In this state we are vulnerable to the dejection which swept over Hamlet when he exclaimed, 'How stale, flat and unprofitable seem to me all the usages of this world.'

Ash Wednesday invites us to resist the pressure of the passing moment, to acknowledge those parts of our life which have become stale and to open ourselves to the gift which Christ longs to impart: newness of life, the gift of the Easter or resurrection life.

The Gospel helps us to see how we should go about our work. The account of the woman caught in adultery in John (8.1–11) does not appear in the very earliest manuscripts, and in the Greek versions of the New Testament it was not finally accepted in the standard text until about 900 AD. The story seems, however, to be ancient and consistent with the teaching of Jesus; but perhaps the early Church was disconcerted by the ease with which Jesus forgave the woman caught in adultery at a time when the Church's own penitential discipline was very stern.

Jesus comes into the Temple very early in the morning. The people come to him and then the religious professionals, the party of the pious enter; we can imagine, with a great surge of indignation. A woman had been caught in adultery: it is important to remember that in the religious law of the time, adultery was unfaithfulness on the part of a married woman. The law was not concerned with affairs between husbands and unmarried women.

The woman had been taken 'in the very act'. She should be stoned: Moses says so in the law. What do *you* say? It is trap of course to show Jesus up as someone with no respect for the law of Moses. You can feel the indignation, the cunning, the fury. Standards slipping everywhere and this so-called teacher undermining the traditions of the faith.

What does Jesus do? He stoops and, with his finger, writes upon the ground.

It is easy to get on a treadmill of over-consumption, overwork, gusts of anger and diminishing awareness. There are warning signs in our irritation within, evidence that there are unacknowledged shadows we are covering up. We relieve the pressure by projecting these shadows on to other people. We do not know what we are doing, but if you have ever felt a surge of dislike for someone you have only just met, hang on to that feeling, for you have been given a precious indication of what you are covering up inside yourself. We all dislike most in others what we are prone to ourselves.

Jesus detaches himself from the confrontation. He stoops rather than bristle and enter into argument. He doodles with his finger upon the earth: perhaps he was acting out the saying of the prophet Jeremiah, 'Those who turn away from you shall be written upon the earth for they have forsaken the Lord, the fountain of living water' (17.13).

The message here is not that we should opt out of confrontations, which may be sometimes necessary, but that if we want to see clearly and engage profoundly there are times when we must stoop down. You disengage to clarify and connect at depth.

What does this mean for us? Awareness is diminished by over-stimulation. Our Lenten fasting should not be some token abstinence from sweeties but a conscious effort to reduce stimulation to stoop to clarify and connect. If we wish to emancipate ourselves from the hectic hype and pressure of the passing moment, then it may be more important to refrain from switching on the *Today* programme first thing in the morning than renouncing chocolate. But do not neglect the reality that what we eat and drink does have a bearing on our awareness and that we often over-indulge because we are unhappy and need to confront that unhappiness.

Jesus's life was marked by a rhythm of walking and talking with the crowds and then retreating to a desert place. In Lent we stoop down and detach in order to clarify and connect more profoundly. That is why any fasting from over-stimulation must be accompanied by a renewed commitment to meditation, the way in which we clarify the world within and reduce the noise so that we can hear the voice of conscience.

The babble continued: 'they continued asking him', so 'he lifted himself up' (we have a hint here that the journey to Easter will pass through the events of Good Friday where he will draw a new world to himself as he is lifted up upon the cross). This lifting up, like the cross, if we contemplate it, shows us ourselves. In the Gospel story he shows the crowd their inner selves. 'He that is without sin among you cast the first stone.'

We may be surrounded by some really difficult and wrong-headed people, but there will be no spiritual progress until we can rein in our projections and see clearly our own state. Christians must give up self-justification for Lent.

God longs for us to enjoy the new life which bursts from the tomb; but our lives become old, a crust forms over the well-spring at the heart of life where the Holy Spirit flows with inexhaustible vitality, we become mired in cynicism and shallow expectations. The palm crosses from last year have been burnt, here is the ash and soon we shall receive the ash on our foreheads as a sign that the natural life disconnected from the life of the Holy Trinity is bound to a cycle of decay and death, from dust to dust. Openness to the gift of Christ comes when we confront our creatureliness and see clearly that we are not immortal gods but mortal humans. Jesus draws clarity and insight from the earth to which he stoops.

Again he stoops down. He does not argue or feed the frenzy of indignation which swept in with the accused woman. Blessedly, those who are given the gift to see themselves when Jesus lifts himself up can hear the truth, and they in turn detach themselves and leave the scene.

Jesus is left alone with the accused woman. Again Jesus lifts himself up and asks, 'Did no man condemn thee?' She says, 'No man, Lord.' Jesus says, 'Neither do I condemn thee; go thy way, from henceforth sin no more.'

Those who think that the woman has got away with it too easily have not understood the spiritual reality of the story. The woman has not been condemned by others but is confronted with her own promise-breaking and unfaithfulness. To confront the truth about oneself can be agony and physical and mental pain. How can we forgive ourselves? That is often the hardest thing to do. Jesus's words cut like a surgeon's scalpel. There is no condemnation, there is release from self-loathing but there is no fudging – walk on and change. First the release, then the transformation.

Give yourself time to be present in this scene, perhaps changing your position as you look and listen to what Jesus says and does. Be one of the original crowd, enter with the scribes, stand by the woman. This is a time for seeing clearly our evasions, the addictive ways in which we hide from the truth about ourselves, our frailty, our mortality, our meanness and worse. Detach in order to confront these realities. Hear Jesus Christ say even to you and me, 'I do not condemn you, but walk on and accept the transformation which comes to those who turn in my direction and are filled with my Spirit.'

St Paul's Cathedral
Ash Wednesday 2004

4

Lent

One thing I know, that whereas I was blind, now I see. (John 9.25)

This story has always been used at this season of the year as a preparation for Christian baptism. St Augustine said, 'This blind man stands for the human race . . . illumination is faith . . . He washes his eyes in that pool – he was baptized in Christ.'

The artistry with which the story is told is astonishing. St John draws portraits of increasing insight on the part of the man blind from birth, and hardening unawareness on the part of his religious interrogators. Three times the former blind man, who is truly gaining knowledge, humbly confesses his ignorance: 'Whether I be a sinner I know not, one thing I know, that whereas I was blind, now I see.' Three times, the Pharisees, who are really plunging deeper into ignorance about Jesus, make confident statements about him.

The climax of the story falls a little outside the passage we have just heard, when the blind man says, 'Lord I believe' and 'he worshipped him'.

The intricacies and craft of the story are such that I could not do justice to this passage in under a two-hour sermon. May I therefore recommend to those who want to explore further in St John the most sane and authoritative commentary by an American scholar, Raymond Brown in the *Anchor Bible* series?

Once again the theme is the light that shines in the darkness and indeed triumphs over the darkness. Jesus acts out 'I am the light of the world', the truth he had proclaimed in Chapter 8. But how are we to gain entry to the spiritual reality of this beautiful old master? We can appreciate the depiction of the blind guides, the religious authorities who make confident assertions about what they know while they are all the time very far from the truth – we are comfortably familiar with them in a way that may even deepen our own unawareness.

How can we identify the darkness in our own time? If we are really to travel on this Lenten journey, then we first have to be aware of the darkness.

It is very simple to begin – first of all we must wake up to where we are. That is why Jesus mixes mud and humus with spittle and anoints the eyes of the blind man. We begin with what surrounds us and where we are without hastening to judgement; remember, the blind man advanced in insight as he remained humble and clear about what he knew and what he didn't.

In waking up and being aware of where we find ourselves this Lent, we have been given some signs and portents.

In the last month of 2001, a work exhibited at Tate Britain won the £20,000 Turner Prize. Work 227 was produced by Martin Creed. There was a white gallery with a handful of light bulbs flickering on and off. It is the most minimal work ever to win the Turner Prize. It is not my intention to line up with 'Disgusted of Tunbridge Wells'. The Tate Communications Curator comments, 'Creed has said that we live in a world full of objects. He wants to make art that does not contribute to that clutter.' I can understand that, and so the lights go on and off in an empty room. It helps us to understand where we are – close to running out of anything to celebrate in a glare that is next door to darkness.

Then again I have also been struck by the immense enthusiasm expressed by sophisticated City workers for the Harry Potter films and *The Lord of the Rings*.

Asking gently about the reasons for this adult passion, I have been told again and again that people experience a sense of absence in their lives, the absence of depth and mystery. How is it that Christians have so obscured the fellowship of the Mystery that good people are enraptured with the fantasy *Fellowship of the Ring* or want to try the Hogwarts entrance exam?

So these are some signs and portents which help us to understand where we are, trapped on the surface of things at a point where meaning and delight seem to be exhausted. It is a place where we do not seem to have the resources within ourselves to do much more than flick from channel to channel watching the repeats or turn the lights on and off.

At some point in life searchers in all ages become aware of spiritual malnutrition. We are programmed to live as if the most real thing in the world were the shell of the surface self we have constructed for ourselves as life has gone on.

All human beings emerge from an experience of one-ness with the source of life, but very early on (this is the significance of the fact that the man had been blind from birth) we set to work subconsciously building a shell for protection and a surface self so that we can negotiate with the world around us. Gradually the experience of oneness with the well-spring of life is lost, a crust forms over our deepest self (a crust of unawareness which is often described in spiritual terms as blindness) and we come to operate more and more from what we have constructed, from the shell, the false self.

Alas, since our true life and our deepest self flows from the source of All Being, the mystery of God (as Psalm 100 says, 'it is he that hath made us and not we ourselves') the effect of operating from the shell of our surface self is, in the end, exhaustion and a sense of absence. This we try to fill with hectic over-activity. The darkness in our own time is accompanied by a loss of rhythm, light and shade in the day and in the year as we seek to have perpetual carnival with no ensuing season of Lent.

This is the great spiritual question, reconnecting ourselves as we are now with the source of true life and vitality. St John says, 'In him was life, and the life was the light of men and the light shineth in the darkness' (John 1.4–5).

The God who revealed himself as 'I am', the name he disclosed to Moses, true Being, does not come or com-municate as a dominator with an iron law. Laws are necessary in this fallen world, but they can react with our personality-building to produce an even more brittle way of being in the world. Being, the Source of

24

Life, the Great I Am, Almighty God, comes in the person of one who spat upon the ground and made clay of the spittle, to invite us, entice us into connectedness.

Those who are bound up with the surface self they have so painfully constructed are contemptuous or afraid like the Pharisees. They seek to destroy the One who proclaims with his life, death and resurrection, that you come to God by subtraction and humility rather than by addition and inflation. 'The world was made by him and the world knew him not' (John 1.10).

'But as many as received him, to them gave he power to become children of God' (John 1.12). If you are prepared to receive sight and know that you are blind, then there is a gift here for you. God has opened a way to reconnect with life in all its fullness and delight.

The spiritual practice of the inner journey is hard and the dangers great, but the joy of seeing draws us on, although at times it is impossible to distinguish the joy from the agony.

When I was young I knew everything. It was very exhausting. I was constantly defending my castle walls, labelling and judging what lay outside.

Opposition hardened my position, but as George Herbert says in his great poem, 'Love bade me welcome' and miraculously found a way through the defences. Jesus Christ, in his life and living Spirit, glimpsed in scriptures and in life, showed me that you must give self away in order to grow in soul.

The crust once breached, I found that there was an answering call from within where the spiritual heart is in each one of us, where there is a centre deep within which connects with the centre of everything that lives.

I have found that simple way of prayer taught by John Main, one of the spiritual explorers of our own generation, very helpful in widening the breach. A period morning and evening in simple contemplation. I was tired of continually instructing God in his duties. Gradually I can see more light which does not come from my own generator but is the uncreated light. I could tell you how often I had been fooled and slipped back into my old ways and rebelled against the simplicity of it all, but that would be another two-hour sermon, and you cannot bear it now. Suffice it to say that once you have glimpsed the true light, the false glamour of the neon strip is revealed and you cannot be satisfied with anything else.

Truly this is a door into a new way of being in the world. One thing I know: that whereas I was blind, now I see.

St Bride's, Fleet Street
10 March 2002

5

Palm Sunday

How do you build a heaven on earth? The modern recipe has had a considerable measure of success. You look for leadership, some outstanding character: a man on a white horse, certainly not a man on an unheroic donkey. You define the problem, you sack the old management, a revolution may be necessary, and then you change the educational curriculum and bring up new resources.

Much has been achieved following this pattern, but there are resistances. Part of the power of the Passion story is that it sheds light on these resistances and then releases energy for a new approach.

Given the choice, you notice, the people call for the release of Barabbas, who, the other Gospels suggest, was a violent revolutionary. His name actually means, ironically, Son of the Father. In his case it was a question of a 'chip off the old block'. Barabbas stood for a reversal of political roles but no profound change in the system of control.

Pilate has no real conviction in the guilt of Jesus, but he gives in to the crowd and releases Barabbas. It is very familiar. It is what happens when the system and its preservation becomes a god.

When something gets put in the place of God, the sign is a taste of untruth in the soul, a sense of anxiety; I suppose that today most obviously it is the economy that is discussed without much relation to the human or the divine. Every morning on the news bulletins, in a quasi-religious incantation, the temperature of our god is taken. The Dow Jones is down ten, the Hang Seng continues its inexorable fall, the Footsie has bounced back.

People reveal their anxiety and the taste of untruth and unease in the soul by cursing the victim who has given them such uncomfortable thoughts. Even those who were crucified with him swore at him. Here we switch from resistances which operate at the macro-level, systems which become gods – things St Paul called 'principalities and powers' – and we get more personal.

'Life in all its fullness', which Jesus said it was his work to open up for us, comes not from attachment to any mere thing but from a relationship freely chosen with God and God's Spirit housed in other people and even deep down in our truest self. Whenever we are alienated from the current of energy and compassion which flows in this relationship then we experience a loss of depth and sap in life.

We try to fill the hole with hectic over-activity which seems to be built on the idea that the faster we live the more we get out of this brief life. We are haunted by the repressed fear of death. We come to experience the world as godforsaken and see ourselves as godforsaken. We internalize the picture of human beings communicated by bad science under the pious rhetoric of human dignity. We come to think of ourselves as rapacious bipeds whose principal function is as a conduit of genetic information from generation to generation.

Jesus, the human face of God, experienced the full weight of this God-forsakenness in that last intelligible cry on the cross using words from Psalm 22: 'My God, my God, why have you forsaken me?'

William Blake says that 'we are put upon this earth a little space to learn to bear the beams of love'. This current of divine love is what quickens our deepest and truest selves, but we are at work from earliest years building a false front for ourselves so that we can survive in the threatening world that actually exists. There comes a point, however, when this crust, this false self, this mask, becomes literally life-leaching.

If we have any inkling of this then this Holy Week is the time to slow down and take some time to contemplate this death – like those women who had followed Jesus from their home in Galilee, who watched him and his death 'from afar'.

The cross is the shape imposed upon perfect love in this world which is organized to resist divine love. If once we see the depth of that in the human face of God with the eyes of our spirit, then the shock reverberates through the crust that has been formed over the years (earthquake is not too strong a word). The centurion said, 'Truly this was the Son of God.' If we can, by the power of God, feel the weight and truth of those words then we shall find that God himself is quickening our deepest and truest selves – souls created to know and participate in the divine life.

All Saints, Fulham
24 March 2002

6

Three Hours at the Cross: The Meditations

> Is it not evident that the Father accepted the sacrifice, not because he demands it or feels some need of it, but in order to carry out his own plans? Humanity had to be brought to life by the humanity of God . . . we had to be called back to him by his Son. Let the rest be adored in silence.
>
> *Gregory Nanzianzen*

Meditation 1:
The new community and its disintegration

'Who are you looking for?' So says Jesus Christ to those who come to arrest him; but it is a question for us as well.

It is a question which echoes through the Gospel of St John. Right at the beginning, Andrew and a companion fall into conversation with Jesus and his first words to them are, 'What are you looking for?' Then near the end, in the garden close by the tomb, Jesus meets Mary Magdalene and asks her, 'Who are you looking for?'

I imagine that we are all here as seekers, but perhaps our questions are not very clear. A time of 'sick hurry and divided aims' in which enlightenment, like the stars in the London sky, is often blocked out by the neon glare, can leave us confused and vaguely dissatisfied. As one of the cast in the poet Auden's 'The Age of Anxiety' says, 'Does your self like mine, Taste of untruth?'

'It's not the feeling of anything I've ever done,' says another character, this time in Eliot's *The Cocktail Party*:

> It's not the feeling of anything I've ever done
> Which I might get away from, or of anything in me
> I could get rid of – but of emptiness, of failure
> Towards someone, or something, outside of myself
> And I must feel I must – atone – is that the word?

Looking beyond ourselves this Good Friday, we see a world of plenty where we have enough food to feed everybody on the planet but often lack the will. We see a world of huge technological progress – not least in the production of 'smart' weapons where there are millions seeking a place of safety from conflict. We see the evidence of hatred so intense that people are prepared to destroy themselves to demolish the Twin Towers and kill fellow human beings inside. As the church bells ring in the Holy Land today they are drowned out by the sound of gunfire.

We come therefore this Good Friday simply to allow the story of Jesus Christ's final hours to sink into us: to see if, without working ourselves into some self-induced state of spiritual excitement, there may be light and even revelation for us here.

The events which we are considering have a firm anchorage in history, but revelation is not so much related to acquiring new facts but rather of seeing and experiencing in a new light. Revelation can illuminate and transform our loves, through the channels of energy opened by the Holy Spirit, as we encounter Jesus Christ and see him as the light of the world. His story begins to make sense of the riddle of our own story and then we begin to feel his life in us.

Jesus begins with his friends crossing the Kidron stream and entering the garden. John has taught us to listen to the themes in the symphony of scripture, and the thought of the Paradise Garden, conjuring up the place where the tragedy of the first human beings unfolded, alerts us to the approaching crisis.

The Gospel has already shown us the response of Jesus Christ to the question, 'What are you looking for?' The root of the dissatisfaction and the lethal conflicts which fuel this question has been uncovered in an event which in St John's story happens close to the beginning of Jesus's work. Christ drives the traders out of the Temple: 'He poured out the changers' money and overthrew their tables . . . and said, "Make not my Father's house, a house of merchandise".'

We should not draw the sting of this episode by supposing that it is merely a swingeing condemnation of cathedral shops. It is a declaration that when things and the relation between things are of primary importance; when human relations occupy a subordinate or dependent position; when even the relationship with God has to be negotiated with things – religious taxes and offerings – then the result is estrangement. God and human beings are estranged from one another and even from their true, their deepest selves. That is why so many people experience 'the taste of untruth'. They experience alienation, which means being a stranger to our own good.

In any organism, staleness and anaemia can only be healed by fresh life-giving energies. The New Testament paints a picture of human beings alienated from life in all its fullness. Ironically this is as a result of a process of self-aggrandizement, constructing a false self and turning away from a free, direct and intimate relationship with God in an act of self in-turning which breeds conflict with other atomized beings.

The whole life of Jesus Christ represents the entry of God into this estrangement in quite a new way. This is no forced entry, but rather he comes as a child born in lowly company in Bethlehem.

The cosmos which had become disordered by man's self in-turning and self-aggrandizement can only be restored to its true goal by an all-embracing representative act of self-outpouring and self-sacrifice. Jesus made this self-offering having identified himself with us, and in doing so opened the channel through which life in all its fullness can flow. God was in Christ reconciling the world unto himself (2 Corinthians 5.19).

'What are you looking for?' may be a good question at the beginning of a spiritual journey, but as the way unfolds it becomes clearer that the question really ought to be, 'Who are you looking for?' Jesus Christ says, 'I came that they may have life and may have it abundantly' (John 10.10).

Life does not consist in the multiplicity of things, or even of religious ideas to which we have become attached; but the real bread of abundant life is the 'I am', True Being, the name which God revealed to Moses and the name which reverberates through all those references in the Gospel to Jesus. 'I am the bread of life'; 'I am the way'; 'I am the truth.'

At this moment of crisis in the garden, Jesus said, 'Who are you looking for?' They answered him, 'Jesus of Nazareth.' Jesus said to them, 'I am he.'

The words actually used in the Greek, '*Ego eimi*', can mean simply, 'It is I', but they are also an echo of the divine name. In the previous chapter, Jesus had celebrated a last meal with his friends before washing their feet and promising them the gift of the Holy Spirit. He then offered a prayer. 'I made known unto them thy name and will make it known; that the love wherewith thou lovedst me may be in them and I in them.'

God is the source of the distinctive quality of human beings which makes for fullness of life, and this consists essentially in the capacity to respond to God's invitation to conscious relationship.

To know the divine name, which for the ancients meant not only to know but to have access to the one named, is to dispose of immense power; and in the garden, even the soldiers and the police backed off.

Jesus had gathered a band of men and women around him who were learning a new kind of abundant life together in a community nourished by a spirit of love, which was not merely an ideal but which dwelt in them and among them. This love transcended all barriers of race, kinship or status and flowed through Christ from the Father, the originator of all fullness, creativity and unity. The disciples were Christ's students in this divinely constituted new society.

His teaching was conveyed with laser-like intensity in the washing of his disciples' feet. Love was to be saved from sentiment by taking the form of service. 'I have given you an example that you should do as

I have done for you . . . By this shall everyone know that you are my disciples, that you love one another' (John 13.15, 35).

All this would amount to little more than utopian daydream without the transforming energy which flows from a new intimacy with God. He taught his pupils to put aside the identities created by defining ourselves over against other people. So close to the Father's heart himself that he could use the divine name 'I am', True Being, he opened a door so that his pupils were equipped to pray, 'Our Father.' Forgive us as we forgive them that trespass against us. Let go anger and disappointment. These are the preconditions for being built up in the great command to love God and our neighbours as ourselves.

So we have been given a diagnosis of what has produced 'our taste of untruth' and our state of conflict. We are intended to enjoy fullness of life but we are going the wrong way about it. We have also been shown a fresh vision of human community as it was intended to be, according to the Maker's instructions.

But what went wrong? The new community disintegrated in the garden where Jesus was arrested. The agent of the betrayal was one of his followers and table companions. We must confront the mystery and the strength of the resistances both within and without to the realization of the divine intention.

Meditation 2:
The Powers of this world

Jesus stands alone before Pilate. The community he had been building as a new way of being in the world disintegrated. They all forsook him and fled. Peter, the

Rock, had even denied that he knew him. Jesus is left alone with the powers that rule this present age. We shall be shown aspects of our world which frustrate the creation of the new community and something of the strength of the resistances which have to be overcome.

John invites us to see Pilate, representative of real-politik, shuttling in and out of the palace. From the presence of Jesus, to the crowds and the chief priests who are waiting outside. It is as if he is shuttling between light and darkness, looking for a way to evade a decision.

John's picture of Pilate does not portray him as a spectacularly wicked man. It will not do for us to project our indignation on to him. Like many of us, he is a prisoner of the system, and in some ways the system Pilate represented had much to recommend it. Roman law and government united the whole Mediterranean world and guaranteed a standard of peace and prosperity throughout the region which was not attained again until the nineteenth century.

The chief priests also were guardians of a highly developed moral tradition and a noble national story. Both the Jewish Establishment and the Roman Procurator were playing an ancient political game, disposing of a disturber of the *status quo*, without being too delicate about the means.

Meanwhile, the crowd also called for the release of Barabbas in preference to Jesus. Barabbas means literally 'son of the father', a chip off the old block, whom other Gospel writers describe as a violent revolutionary. Like revolutionaries through the ages, however, Barabbas stood for a reversal of political roles but no profound change in the system of control and domination. We learnt the hard way throughout the last century that new commissar is just old czar writ large and even more ruthless.

It is all so credible; this is the world we know, this is our world. There are areas of relative peace and plenty preserved by a superiority of force which excludes the other world of need and insecurity. This is a world in which we have enough food to ensure that everyone is fed, but we do not have the will. This is a world in which the 40 richest people dispose of more wealth than the poorest 40 per cent of the world's population. This is a world of huge achievements and certainly preferable to a state of disorder and chaos. But this is also a world maintained at a cost to the poor and repression of their attempts to revise their status.

This is the world so familiar to us that our Lord entered. The word of God coming into the world did not merely go about telling people to be nice to one another. Jesus Christ gave people an inkling of their true nature and began to gather around him a new community. It was non-violent and inclusive, a community in which human beings would see and serve their deepest selves in one another because they had been caught up by Jesus to his level of awareness, close to the heart of the Father.

This truly revolutionary social enterprise amounted to a new creation, and the powers which dominate the world as we know it recognized the threat which Jesus and his kingdom posed.

Pilate asked Jesus whether he was truly a king. Jesus had always been wary of that title. When, as John describes in chapter 6, Jesus realized that the people were intent on making him a king, he fled to the mountain. His kingship and kingdom are not according to the model offered by the world as it is now. Always he struggled to prevent people misunderstanding the nature of the gifts he offered. The light, bread and kingship he offered, were charged with a 'truth', reality, because they issued from God and were distinct from the things those words signified in an unblessed life.

Our world is dominated by Powers, a word used in the epistles of St Paul to designate the world rulers of this present age. These are not so much individuals but spirits, the cravings and fears which have their greatest influence in the sphere of the false self which has been built between our true selves and God.

Ironically, Pilate identifies Jesus as a guiltless king, but he fails to decide for him and shuttles outside the palace again where the crowd is howling for blood. Like a prudent administrator, he gives way.

Jesus Christ is the light of the world, and in his Passion story he unmasks the Powers and reveals the character of this world, the world in which we live, where high ideals mix with reasons of state. Reasons of state demand that blood should be taken. The world Jesus is building is founded on blood given. Pilate shuttles back and forth, between the light of the world and the crowd, trying to evade a decision.

This Good Friday, who could fail to see that a decision is urgently required? With the growing interconnectedness of all things, with a global economy and communications system, we are searching for a new kind of human community in which we do not define ourselves over against others. We know that the penalty for failure is that human beings will sooner or

later unleash the mushroom cloud that we have con-
jured up and destroy themselves. The call to our
generation is insistent but consistently ignored. We
must work urgently for one world or face the possibility of no world.

We have been given two signs, revealed to the post-
World War generation and to no previous generations.
The signs are the mushroom cloud which brings
darkness at noon, and the earth seen for the first time
from outer space – a single globe, bathed in light,
sapphire blue and beautiful. That is the choice which
confronts us – the cloud or the globe. Jesus Christ, the
light of the world, in his confrontation with the Powers
on Good Friday reveals the need for a decision.

Meditation 3:
The cross
Jesus Christ was not crucified between two candle-
sticks on an altar, but he was tortured to death in the
way that Romans reserved for rebels. Even the ancient
world, which had a stronger stomach for public horrors
than ours, regarded crucifixion as a peculiarly terrible
punishment.

Wordy meditations about the body of Jesus Christ
hanging on the cross will not get us very far and may
even anaesthetize the moment. We must quieten ourselves down and pray at this point, as the ancient
writers say, 'with the mind in the heart'.

Lord, give us grace to see that pity wailing over
suffering is not love, that weeping without
penitence is not life, unless they lead to action,
the giving of ourselves to serve and suffer for the

40

loved. Lord, give us understanding of your way,
lead us to know the mystery of your pain, that we
may follow you and plead with you in this your
sacrifice and enter in the gate of love to walk
love's way. (after Fr Gilbert Shaw)

Those to be crucified were, like Jesus, commonly
beaten up and stripped. They were then nailed to a
cross about seven feet tall so that the wild animals
could leap up to the body. It was all so easy, as we can
see from the narrative, for passers-by to mock the
figure hanging on the cross only just above their
heads. Death was often a long time in coming.

He was mocked, 'Thou that destroyest the temple
and buildest it in three days, save thyself.' The Temple
was the central symbol of the old order. It was not only
a place of worship but the pinnacle of a system of social
and economic organization which benefited some, but
by no means all. Jesus had wryly observed this by
sitting 'over against the treasury' when he noted that
while the rich gave out of their superfluity, the widow
had to contribute all her living.

The new community was not to be centred on this
great institution, constructed on its mountain, but on
the body of Jesus Christ.

There is no lack of realism in the teaching of Jesus
about the difficulties to be overcome in building the
new human community, the new Israel. Above all, he
taught that the obstacle to entering this new reality is
attachment to the surface self, the clothed self that we
have manufactured as our way of negotiating with the
world around us.

Modern people often call this surface self, the ego. It

is the self which is organized over against other selves, and regards and negotiates with the others as with objects to be managed.

All human beings emerge from an experience of oneness with the source of life, but very early on set to work subconsciously building a shell for protection and a surface self so that we can negotiate with the world around us. Gradually the experience of oneness with the well-spring of life is lost, a crust forms over our deepest self and we come to operate more and more from what we have constructed, from the shell, the false self. At this level, we are largely unaware of the influences, the cravings and the fears which form a zone of drives and complexes just beneath the surface of the crust, the carapace we have formed. The more unaware we are of this zone, the more enthralled to it we are.

The great spiritual question is how we can reconnect ourselves as we are now with the source of true life and vitality. St John says, 'In him was life and the life was the light of men and the light shineth in the darkness' (John 1.4–5).

True Being, the Source of Life, the Great 'I am', Almighty God, comes in the person of the crucified to invite us, to entice us to connectedness.

Those who are bound up with the surface self that they have so painfully constructed, are contemptuous. They hurl abuse, not knowing that what they are saying is the plain truth. He is the true King. 'He saved others, himself he cannot save.' 'The world was made by him and the world knew him not.' Even those who were crucified with him jeered at him, enemies to their own good.

'But as many as received him, to them gave he power to become children of God' (John 1.12). If we are prepared to receive, then there is a gift here for us. God has opened a way to reconnect with life in all its fullness and delight, although the journey to our spiritual centre through the zone dominated by cravings and fear is hard and dangerous.

The manufacture of the false self is part of the human condition, and every one of us is involved in this work to survive and function. Spiritual growth, however, at a certain point in life demands a reversal and a progressive diminution of the ego so that our true selves can be liberated and flourish.

Adam and Eve hide themselves from the Lord God in the Garden of Eden, clothing themselves to hide from God, but Jesus is stripped and naked to God on the cross. William Blake said, 'We are put upon this earth a little space to learn to bear the beams of love.' Alas, we are hard at work from earliest years to build beam-proof shelters; and from this position, as the psalmist says, 'no man hath quickened his own soul'.

The soul is the full expression of our deepest self which was created for communion with God and all other beings, created by God. The soul thrives in connection and communion. The ego is oriented towards self-preservation by domination.

The ego regards the world around as composed of objects of its thought or desire. The deepest self, the spiritual heart, sees other subjects. That is why, in what he says and what he does, in how he lives and in how he dies, our Lord teaches that 'whosoever would save his life shall lose it and whosoever shall lose his life for my sake and the gospel's shall save it' (Mark 8.35).

If we dwell in our surface self, building our castle walls to defend ourselves against others and constructing a position from which we can control the surrounding landscape, then cut off from the freely given and received exchange of love and worth which is the source of the profoundest energy in life, and feeding on the poison of the cravings and fears which lie hidden just beneath the surface, we shrink. In the end our defence becomes our undoing.

This truth is hidden from those who pass by and mock. The body of Jesus, the centre of the new community, hangs upon the cross. It appears that the Powers have won and that there will be no new spring for the world. 'Let Christ the King of Israel now come down from the cross that we may see and believe. And they that were crucified with him, reproached him' (Mark 15.32).

Meditation 4:
The veil

The sixth hour was, in Roman reckoning, noon. There was darkness at noon, just as, when Jesus was born, there was brightness at midnight. The sun, so often the symbol of imperial power, was eclipsed.

It was a moment prophesied by Amos: 'In that day saith the Lord GOD, that I will cause the sun to go down at noon, and I will darken the earth in the clear day . . . I will make it as the mourning of an only son and the end thereof as a bitter day' (Amos 8.9–10).

The Gospel began with the voice of one crying in the wilderness, the prophet John the Baptist, whose end was to be killed by Herod. Now, at what seems to be the end, there is one last cry, a terrible cry using words from the beginning of Psalm 22: 'My God, my God, why hast thou forsaken me?' Jesus feels the full weight of the God-forsakenness which there is in the world in thrall to the Powers. 'My God' is an unusual beginning prayer for Jesus. His own prayers began with the intimate, 'Abba, Father.' But 'Eloi . . .' is the Aramaic version of Psalm 22, not the Hebrew. We are close to the very words of Jesus himself, an Aramaic speaker.

Some among the bystanders, like people throughout the history of the Church, have not given up hope of a happy ending, the arrival of some celestial fifth cavalry so that we might be shielded from the dreadful truth that the passage to new life goes through suffering by accepting death.

Some of them stood by and said, 'Behold he calleth Elijah.' But we know from Jesus himself that Elijah has already come in the person of John the Baptist and has been spurned. Once again Jesus uttered a loud voice and gave up the ghost.

We enter eternal life by coming to our senses, by staying here today; by becoming aware not least of death. So much about the way we live now, the hectic pace which seems to be based on the logic that the faster we live, the more we will get out of this short life, flows from a repressed fear of death which stalks this civilization. The cross stands for the truth, that we can only enter life in all its fullness by embracing our own death. Christians through the ages have discovered that this is not a morbid path but the very opposite. To accept and to be aware of our own death is a liberation which enables us to stand beside others in a deeper way.

The message is even deeper than that of course. We

are summoned to enter into the great exchange of love which gives and receives in freedom rather than buys or sells; which contemplates with joy rather than consumes to the point of satiation.

Our contemplation includes the cost. In so many ways we discover that real love lies in the letting go. This is an agonizing experience for anyone who has loved deeply. We also discover that with non-possessive love you make a gift of power to the other person which exposes you to deep injury and wounds. Jesus Christ teaches us this truth as he hangs silently on the cross.

The way opened up by our Lord discloses that if you do set out to make your neighbour your work of art in the new human community which Jesus came to inaugurate, then you will be exposed to hurt and unimaginable pain. But as you look deeply into the human face of God, he will awake and strengthen your deepest self which was made in his image; he will quicken your soul. This is work we cannot do for ourselves – it is beyond our strength and imagining. Jesus Christ lifted up upon the cross is the mirror in which we glimpse our true God-created selves. Jesus Christ is the true self of the human race.

It appears that the Powers have had the last word. The body which was to have been the heart of the new community falls silent. But immediately (Mark's favourite word), the veil before the Holy of Holies in the Temple, the great symbol of the old order, is split from top to bottom, torn like the wineskins when the new patch is applied or like the garments of the High Priest when he was confronted by Jesus. The rending of the veil is towards the end of the story which began with the rending of the heavens and God's intervention. Now the sanctuary is evacuated as the veil is rent.

The fury of the Powers has brought their world to the edge of destruction.

Jesus hangs on the cross in silence, and a great tempest of hate and violence rages around him. It is a revelation of the true nature of the Powers and an explosion which brings them closer to exhaustion and bankruptcy. Jesus takes upon himself all this pain and anger without reinvigorating it by returning railing for railing and cursing for cursing. Instead he takes it into himself, although the cost is terrible – 'My God, my God, why hast thou forsaken me?'

To those who pass by, such a death means nothing or is simply a disgusting spectacle. The gospel is revealed, however, not so much to spectators and commentators but to followers, learners, disciples in the new community which Jesus, the true self of the human race, inaugurates. We are to become the body of Jesus in the world, Jesus who himself embodies the life for others which is the true vocation of human beings made in the image of God. In the words of St Gregory Nazianzen, 'Humanity had to be brought to life by the humanity of God . . . we had to be called back to him by his Son.'

We contemplate the cross of Jesus Christ this afternoon in the light of the responsibility which the climax of the story as St Mark presents it places upon us. A splendid reversal of the victory claimed by the exhausted and discredited Powers would have been one thing, but this insistence that the person awakened by the self-sacrifice of Jesus Christ can only begin again, wherever they are, to follow him as a servant, offering life so as to enter into life more profoundly – this is deeply disturbing. It is no wonder that this message caused wonder and astonishment to fall upon the women who were to find the tomb empty. 'They said nothing to anyone for they were afraid.' That is where the ancient texts of St Mark's Gospel ended.

Meditation 5:
A fearful hope

The Powers proclaim Jesus even while destroying him; their cynical frankness about Jesus hints at a mysterious pattern in the world where even evil is compelled to serve the Creator's purposes.

For the moment, however, the Powers seem to remain in occupation of the field. The centurion which 'stood over against him' named him, 'Truly this man was the Son of God.' The Powers operating through the demons had always recognized Jesus for who he was, and pronouncing the true name of someone was believed to give power over that person.

But the centurion was not a demoniac, and the veil of the Temple had been torn and the veil of unawareness which still lay over the eyes of the disciples was close to destruction by the shock wave which flowed from such a death.

And there are those women still there, unlike the men because they had not only followed him but served him in Galilee. We wait and watch with them a little while to contemplate the form taken by perfect love when it enters this world of ours.

Holy Trinity Brompton
29 March 2002

7

Good Friday

Towards the end of Bach's *St Matthew Passion* we hear, with an intensity deepened by Bach's music, the centurion say, 'Truly this was the Son of God.' Witnessing the reverberations of this death on the cross, even an officer of the occupying power recognizes Jesus Christ as the human face of God.

Earthquake is not too strong an image of the reality of this breakthrough into awareness. William Blake said, 'We are put upon this earth a little space to learn to bear the beams of love.' Alas, we are hard at work from earliest years to build beam-proof shelters, and from this position no man, as the Psalm says, 'hath quickened his own soul'.

The manufacture of this shelter which hardens into a false self is part of the human condition. Every one of us has to do this work to survive and function, but spiritual growth at a certain point in life demands a reversal and a progressive diminution of the egoistical false self so that our true selves may be liberated and flourish.

The surface self, however necessary its construction, once achieved, is a barrier between our deepest selves and God; a barrier which in the end prevents growth and interrupts the healthy and energizing exchange of love which is intended to pass between the heart of our being and the heart of God.

We enter eternal life by attending to the Passion, by coming to our senses, by staying here today; by becoming aware not least of death. So much about the way we live now, the hectic pace which seems to be based on the logic that the faster we live the more we will get out of this short life, flows from a repressed fear of death which stalks this civilization. The cross stands for the truth that we can only enter life in all its fullness by embracing our own death. Christians through the ages have discovered that this is not a morbid path but the very opposite. To accept and be aware of our own death is a liberation which enables us to stand beside others in a deeper way.

The message is even deeper than that of course. We are summoned to enter into the great exchange of love which gives and receives in freedom rather than buys or sells; which contemplates with joy rather than consumes to the point of satiation.

Our contemplation includes the cost. In so many ways we discover that real love lies in the letting go. This is an agonizing experience for anyone who has loved deeply. We also discover that with non-possessive love you make a gift of power to the other person which exposes you to deep injury and wounds. Jesus Christ teaches us this truth as he hangs silently on the cross.

Sometimes he sends the gift of tears so that the heart of stone can become once more the heart of flesh. Then we shall know the reality of the pictures given to us in Exodus of how the water gushes out of the heart of the flinty rock. Sometimes he sends a burning love and we understand how the bush which Moses saw burns with fire but is not consumed.

As you look deeply into the human face of God, he will awaken and strengthen your deepest self which was made in his image, he will quicken your soul. This is work we cannot do for ourselves, it is beyond our strength and our imagining.

'All they that go down into the dust shall kneel before him; and no man hath quickened his own soul . . . The heavens shall declare his righteousness unto a people that shall be born, whom the Lord hath made' (Psalm 22. 29, 31).

You sometimes hear preachers say that the cross is 'I' crossed out. But this is only half the story, and if misunderstood this teaching of the 'I' crossed out can lead to a self-lacerating, not a liberating form of religion. Certainly the pain involved in breaking through the crust, which has been so many years in the making, and the peril of journeying to the centre through the zone of the hidden drives and complexes which lies beneath the crust, this pain and peril is inescapable: but beyond lies the promise.

It is summed up by St Bernard: in a very simple way we begin by seeking to come to fulfilment by building ourselves up as we are. We seek fullness of life by addition, by aggrandizement. We begin with 'Love of self for self's sake'.

Even religion can become bent into this pattern and we come to 'Love God for self's sake'.

God can become our possession, our asset; but if we are following the way of Jesus then we risk loving without bargaining, without being like the merchants in the Temple. We pass through the stage of relating to our ideas about God, and turning God into an asset of ours, to the stage where we remain with him even as he cries, 'My God, my God, why hast thou forsaken me?' Then we can come to love the human face of God and 'Love God for God's sake'.

Then as we enter into the soulful life we make a further joyful discovery: 'Love of self for God's sake'. We come back to ourselves, but this time God has restored to us awareness of our true self. We are fearfully and wonderfully made, beings for whose sake Christ shed his life-blood. We cannot estimate ourselves and our neighbours too highly when we reach this state of awareness.

If we are dwelling in the surface self, a lonely atomized individual trying to be satisfied by consuming things and people, then eternal life, life beyond death, is inconceivable, and our fate is to be an actor in a world of conflict. Our birth as a spiritual being, a being whom the Lord in his quickening love has made, this birth is aborted. If we love and serve Christ in our neighbour, inspired by his love lifted up and published on the cross, then we will know pain, but we will grow surer of the reality of God and the immortality of our soul. This is certain and has been proved by saints and martyrs over and over again. To know this is to know the reality of the resurrection.

St George's, Hanover Square
Good Friday 2002

8

Easter (1)

We are accustomed to sing:

> Lo, Jesus meets us, risen from the tomb
> Lovingly he greets us, scattering fear and doom.

But fear and the terror of death are on every side. So says the psalmist, and so says every news broadcaster this Eastertide

Hostages in Iraq with knives held to their throats. Anxiety in cities, as the authorities say, 'Not if, but when' terror will strike. The Easter story is also full of fear. The disciples are behind locked doors, fearful of further action against them. The women in the Gospel who find the tomb empty do not immediately rejoice; they are 'terrified' and fall to the ground.

Fear at root is disconnection with the source of life, a sense of being profoundly at risk. In childhood we find comforters in all kinds of beloved soft toys. In adulthood we lust for success, and status assuages our sense of disconnected powerlessness; collecting precious things ministers to our sense of being value-less; living up to the expectations that others have of us conceals our sense of worthlessness; climbing up mountains responds to our sense of weakness and impotence; over-consuming is a bid to fill the void.

Our hectic lifestyle covers a fear of death. The idea is that the faster we live the more we shall get out of this short life.

Fear is a great black hole at the roots of our being and we seek to pack the hole with all kinds of dream fillings. There comes a time however when the filling cannot conceal the ache and the dread at the heart of our life. We are ready for the journey back to the centre, threading our way through the rubble with which we have filled our sense of loss. We must penetrate the crust and the surface self which we have built up in order to discover our true selves.

This is a hard way; sometimes it seems like the way to the death of all our security – but without the cross there is no crown. Nevertheless, we face great resistance. The false gods of this world turn our fear into violence against others and against ourselves. The suicide bomber unites both violence against others and the self in one act, under the influence of the gods of this world.

The true God whose face Jesus shows us today turns the violence born of fear into suffering love. Perfect love casts out fear.

All through the Gospels we see Jesus's followers hoping and praying that he is going to deal with fear, the fear of individuals and the fear which all peoples experience, the fear of death and extinction of identity by imposing some order which will last for ever. A little later in Luke 24 from which our Gospel is taken, two of his followers confess that 'we hoped that it was he that should redeem Israel'.

There is no way out in this fashion but it was what they were expecting. So earnestly had the disciples hoped for and expected this dramatic reversal of fortune that the sight of the empty tomb and the heavenly messengers evoked terror in the women and amazement from Peter. Faith cannot be deduced from this strange event. The trouble is that we have come to identify with the surface self, sometimes called the personality that we have made for ourselves. It takes time for the true life to make itself felt.

It is only when we come to understand the conversation between God and human beings afresh in light of this resurrection event, when we meditate on the communication of God and try to live out the non-exclusive, suffering love which Jesus embodied and which we practise in the common meal we are celebrating now, that faith is given to us and divisions overcome. This morning when we spilled on to the steps after the dawn breakfast with the risen Jesus, the few people with whom I was able to talk included two Poles from Warsaw, a man from L'vov in the Western Ukraine, someone from Cluj in Transylvania and a yoga teacher from Oslo. Being companions at the table of Jesus Christ re-draws all the maps.

In the passage we heard from the Acts of the Apostles, the Peter who on seeing the empty tomb was merely amazed is discovered seeing 'Him whom God raised up the third day and gave him to be made manifest not to all the people but unto witnesses which were chosen before of God even to us who did eat and drink with him after he rose from the dead' (Acts 10.40–41).

One thing is clear. The record of our community goes

55

beyond anything so trite as the claim that his example lives on in us. Our fear was and is such that only an act of God can unlock the way to reconnect with inexhaustible being.

This way lies open to us this day and I pray that you will be renewed in your desire to follow Jesus's way of non-possessive love. Desire which arises from a sense of deficiency, and a desire to fill that black hole, in the end leads to desperation. Desire awakened by the love of the risen Christ transforms our life into the gold of selfless joy. Jesus in the Holy Spirit holds out the possibility of reconnecting with life in all its fullness and participating in what the springtime Christians called the dance of the Holy Trinity.

If we persevere in his way with our companions around the table then the substitute life we have fabricated for ourselves will dissolve, and what is beyond our manufacture or even imagining will expand and become all in all.

Christ is risen. Hallelujah!

St Paul's Cathedral
Easter 2004

9

Easter (2)

Cleopas said, 'Are you the only stranger in Jerusalem who does not know the things that have taken place there? . . . We had hoped that Jesus was the one to redeem Israel.'

This morning as we gather here in tranquillity in this ancient and beautiful church, the church bells in the Holy Land are being drowned out by the sound of gunfire. In a world of suicide bombers and punitive responses; in a world of hatred so intense that people are willing to sacrifice themselves to destroy the Twin Towers and kill the fellow human beings inside; in a world where precious resources are spent manufacturing 'smart' weapons which nevertheless cannot avoid what is euphemistically called 'collateral damage' how are we to understand, let alone celebrate, the resurrection?

Good Friday is painful enough but we can at least identify with the crucified victim in a world like this. But that is precisely the point of the story we have just heard. Cleopas and no doubt the other disciples had a clear idea of what the work of Jesus was intended to achieve and they had been disappointed. Understandably they were depressed.

In such a mood of disappointed hope and grief we can easily see ourselves in the suffering of the crucified Jesus. The trouble is that seeing ourselves as the victim legitimates our contribution to the chain of violence in which martyrs are avenged by creating new martyrs. The sufferings and injustices are real but can blind us to our share in keeping the old cycles going. The Christian churches have no right to feel smug about this. Catholics and Protestants have glorified their own martyrs – More and Campion, or Latimer and Ridley, depending on which side you are on – and edited out the others. Thank goodness you have shown us a good example here.

The story of Good Friday, however, was much more disturbing than the friends of Jesus might easily admit. Jesus, on the night of the Last Supper, gave himself, body and soul, to his friends gathered in that Upper Room. One of them was an accomplice in his arrest and death and the others also betrayed him by running away. Jesus had opened the door to a new world, a new community nourished by self-giving love, and his closest friends had slipped back into the old world.

One of the common themes in the resurrection appearances is that Jesus Christ surprises his followers and meets them as a stranger. Jesus on the road to Emmaus is greeted as a stranger. Mary mistakes him for the gardener. His former friends have difficulty recognizing him until he takes the initiative and greets them, until he takes bread, blesses and breaks it and gives it to them.

The message is do not fear, and go back either to Galilee where they all came from or to the record of

God's conversation with human beings in the scriptures. In the light of the resurrection of this familiar stranger we come to understand our own stories and those of our families and nations and our own part in Jesus's death. Peter will be asked three times 'Do you love me?' because he has to recognize himself as the one who denied Jesus three times and played his part in betraying him. Facing ourselves and receiving forgiveness for our share in the cycles of violence and cynicism lies behind that phrase in the first letter of St Peter, 'Now that you have purified your souls by obedience to the truth so that you have genuine mutual love.'

This recognition unleashes the energy and power to present Jesus Christ as the hope of the world in the very place and to the very people who were accomplices in killing him. Forgiven himself, Peter has power to address the crowd about Jesus, whom we crucified.

At Easter there is no 'martyr for our cause' to be discovered and no cross that can be used to sanctify an ideology or any particular system. Jesus meets us as a stranger, teaches us to see our complicity in family feuds, political conflict and economic injustice, which in some cases go back centuries.

One of the most unbelievable theories about the resurrection is that it was simply a communal hallucination, wishful thinking. What Jesus's friends were looking for was an event or a person that would fit in with their 'hopes'. They were not reckoning on a 'new birth'.

The Christian community is created by Easter and the resurrection of Christ, not the other way round. We have been shown our 'old self' as St Paul says, but that is not the end of the story. Jesus calls his betrayers his brothers and invites them to go back to their own roots, Galilee, to receive a new self as forgiven people so that they 'might walk in newness of life'. It is Peter the betrayer, the forgiven, who communicates the resurrection to the very people who crucified him in the very place of his death.

If we have really entered into this story, seen the betrayal, watched the crucifixion, gone to the tomb expecting to find a dead hero, and instead heard the Easter shout 'He is not here . . . he is alive', if we have accepted his command to go back to Galilee, our own roots in the everyday, to recognize our old selves but to be freed from ourselves as forgiven people, then we shall know the newness of life, the resurrection life in our deepest God-created selves, and we and our community will be genuine signs of peace and hope, and agents of peace and hope in this world of warring victims.

Easter and the greeting of the risen Christ created the Church. Jesus appears not as some ghostly apparition with instructions for his friends on how to escape this ghastly world. On the contrary, all the stories stress both the initial difficulty his friends had in recognizing him but also they emphasize his presence around a table, on the sea shore, in the locked room where they had gathered.

Jesus had created his new community by speech, touch and the sharing of food. After the resurrection, the forgiven community is sustained in the same way.

By their desertion and their betrayal, the friends of Jesus had ranged themselves on the side of the lost and guilty and made themselves marginal to the new life which Jesus embodied. At Easter, Christ welcomes them and us back to the meal which provides the key to understanding and opening the way to the new life.

At this service we give up our food and drink at the offertory into the hands of Jesus so that we become his guests and receive our life from him. The elements become charged with a new potential because they are no longer our possessions but gifts. In every Eucharist the meaning of the material world is changed from the kind of possession which inevitably gives rise to conflict, to gift which creates the conditions for reconciliation between human beings.

On this Easter morning we celebrate the reversal of death and the open door into fresh hope for the world. Christ is risen. He is risen indeed.

Much Hadham*
14 April 2002

* This venue was a church shared by members of the Church of England and Roman Catholics.

10

Ascension

'Then he opened their minds to understand the scriptures.' Even so, risen Lord Jesus, give us true insight
into your word.

One of the challenges of a bishop's life is the cult of
anniversaries. You not only have to fulfil your own
diary but that of your predecessors as well. Four hundred years ago the Bishop of London, Richard Bancroft
was a participant in the Hampton Court Conference
which made such a significant contribution to developing the identity of the Church of England. The Puritan
delegation had arrived with a number of requests to
King James I. They wanted to abridge 'the longsome-
ness' of the service (to give more time for the sermon)
and to moderate 'to better edification' church songs
and music. They wanted to abolish symbols and
ceremonies like the signing with the cross in baptism.
Vestments were rags of popery, and Mr Knewstubbe,
one of the Puritan delegation, complained about the
surplice which he said had been worn by the priests of
Isis.

There were two different visions of God at the
Conference. For the Puritans, the word in the mind

and the mouth was the way to engage with the rational God. Bodily observances, elaborate music and symbolic communication was a muddying of the waters. Those who wished to retain old ceremonies and symbols in the Church were simply intent on curdling the pure milk of the gospel, obscuring the truth, as Milton later said, with 'guegaws fetcht from Aron's old wardrobe'.

There was another voice – a minority but more musical – within the Jacobean church with a different vision of what God required. One of the most influential of these voices belonged to Launcelot Andrewes who, as Dean of Westminster, was a largely silent but influential participant in the Conference. Like the theologians of the primitive Church, Andrewes and his school believed that God was a mystery to be approached not so much with the word in the mind and the mouth but with the mind in the spiritual heart. One of Andrewes' friends, John Buckeridge, warned that 'true religion is no way a gargleism only, to wash the tongue and mouth, to speak words; it must root in the heart and then fructify in the hand, else it will not cleanse the whole man'.

The Hampton Court Conference ensured that, although the Andrewes line was not the majority one, the door was kept open for a church that respected the ultimate mystery of God, was not ambitious to go beyond scripture and overdefine that mystery, and which respected the symbolic way to the encounter with God.

Actually, without a lively sense of the potential of symbolism it is possible to misinterpret the scriptures in the light of a flatland literalism. Lord, open our minds to understand the scriptures.

The scriptures celebrate the climax of Christ's passage through time, the ascension to the Father 'whom no one hath seen at any time'. The literalist school struggles to be clear about what an observer with a polaroid camera would have seen of the ascension in our Gospel reading. Their embarrassment has led to a neglect of this festival.

A fruitful recent approach has drawn attention to the Temple symbolism, which lies behind much of the New Testament and indeed behind the Christian liturgy. The High Priest entering the Holy of Holies in clouds of incense is the Temple reality, which gives rise to visions of a human figure entering heaven, as in the prophecy of Daniel, or coming down riding on the clouds.

There is hardly a liturgical practice better attested in holy scripture than the use of incense. The legend is that Adam and Eve, when expelled from the Paradise Garden, were able to smuggle out some seeds which they sowed in the world. From these seeds grew the incense-bearing trees, so incense is a lingering perfume of Paradise whereas smoke is what we have made of the world.

The Temple of Jerusalem was seen as a microcosm of the whole creation. The entry of the High Priest into the Holy of Holies on the Day of Atonement and the sacrifice of the substitute beast was the adumbration of the theme later gloriously articulated in the self-offering and self-sacrifice of Jesus Christ.

It used to be said that Jesus had no sense of being the Messiah and that in any case people were not expecting a Messianic figure to appear. The disciples, it was alleged, imposed upon the historical Jesus, the peripatetic healer and prophet, the character of divine saviour. More recent research has opened up a different perspective.

One of the scrolls discovered in the caves near the Dead Sea after the Second World War is the Qumran Melchizedek text, written down about 50 years before the birth of Jesus but possibly not composed at that date. The Melchizedek scroll talks of the return of the High Priest, the new Melchizedek at the beginning of the tenth Jubilee. The Jubilee was used as a measure of time in the period after the building of the Second Temple of Jerusalem, and there is a plausible argument to suggest that the context for the ministry of Jesus was the fervour and expectation of the beginning of the Tenth Jubilee period.

Also, the Melchizedek scroll alludes many times to the Jubilee prophecy in Isaiah 61.1, 'The Lord God has anointed me to bring liberation.' The anointed one in Greek is of course Christos and the prophecy is the one pronounced by Jesus at the beginning of his ministry in the synagogue in Nazareth. The scene is described earlier in Luke's Gospel, when Jesus said, 'Today hath this scripture been fulfilled in your ears.' Once given the key, so much in scripture is bathed in fresh light.

When Luke described the Ascension, he said that Jesus was 'lifted up and a cloud took him'. Jesus was passing beyond the veil, beyond the constraints of time and place, just like the High Priest entering the sanctuary. He was passing into the eternal present beyond and before the creation. That is why he prayed in John's Gospel, 'Father glorify thou me in thy own presence with the glory that I had with thee before the world was made.'

The Temple background to the symbolism is made perfectly clear in the early epistle to the Hebrews.

> But when the Anointed One appeared, the High Priest of good things to come, then through the greater and more perfect tabernacle, not made with hands, that is to say not of this creation, he entered in once and for all into the holy place, not by means of the blood of goats and calves but through his own blood, having obtained eternal redemption. (Hebrews 9.11–12)

There is no ram caught in a thicket to save Isaac from sacrifice, no scapegoat who must bear the sins of the people; Jesus our High Priest who has passed into the heavens has made the sacrifice of his own life and blood. This is my body; this is my blood.

The one who has been lifted up is the channel of renewal. The men in white said that Jesus would return the same way as he had departed. John introduced the book of Revelation with the assurance that 'he is coming with the clouds'. Later, John was granted his own vision of the Lord's return (Revelation 10.1).

Hasty modern folk want to know the 'cash value' of these symbols. Can we distil them into general 'spiritual truths'? These general truths on examination prove to have little transforming power, they lie so easily bedridden in the dormitory of the mind. It is when you enter into the story and see your own story in its light that transforming fission occurs. Here you have a temple where you re-enact this drama of re-membering his body (the opposite of dismembering), lifting up and receiving back the body of Christ. We are called to shape our own lives according to this drama.

But be warned; as you know, this is not play-acting. There is real blood, real sacrifice involved for those who are really open to real presence and the renewal which Christ brings. The drama transforms our lives in every part if only we will allow it entry in to us.

The test is always whether this community is alive in the self-giving love of Jesus Christ. Is this a hot-bed of charity? Do you love one another? Do you love yourselves as persons for whom Christ was content to die? Do you love this parish and those who live here? Do you love and give to the extension of the work of the Church? Do you love and give to the needs of the poor in those areas of the world where Christ is crucified every day? These are the tests.

If we become witnesses of these things as people who have come to live with the mind in the heart, we can hear and believe what the risen Christ says to his students: 'Behold, I send forth the promise of the Father upon you but tarry ye in the city until ye be clothed with power from on high.' If we have the play and no real sacrifice, then we shall have no renewal, no Pentecost, and the Puritans will consider themselves justified.

St John's, Notting Hill
20 May 2004

11

Pentecost

Christ is our future, but where do we find ourselves?

We have lived through a time when the Church worldwide has experienced confusion and violent storms. The twentieth century saw more Christian martyrs than any since the crucifixion. Even in our own relatively tranquil country, the prophet poets describe the spiritual life of our time as 'the waste-land'. Things have grown old and cold; a litter of dead images lies around the cult stone; the stream by the altar of God is very low.

Some of the most popular TV series of the moment are concerned with makeovers and instant trans-formations. *Changing Rooms* and *Ground Force* will deliver a new image in the space of a single pro-gramme. Public figures are also intensely concerned with image and employ spin doctors to make them 'accessible and cuddly'.

Likewise, there is a great preoccupation with the image of the Church and the idea that if we had a makeover, the Church would become more popular again. Worship in particular, we are told, should become more accessible and led by people like you and me in lounge suits. People, we are told, are put off by anything that is difficult to grasp at first hearing.

There are several things wrong with this thesis. It is rather condescending about the capacities of the person in the street to understand where once their wonder is engaged. Anyone who has seen the Pokemon craze sweep through their families knows that even quite young children are able to master biographical details of 150 mutants. They can describe with bewildering specificity the conditions under which Matchoke evolves into Matchamp. Is it really true that they cannot be trusted with anything but a dumbed-down version of the thrilling story of the Ancient of Days, on his throne of fiery flames? (Daniel 7).

At the same time, when we are sleepwalking in the wasteland, anything instantly graspable in such a state is likely to be of very little value in helping us to wake up spiritually. If we want to wake up spiritually to the fullness of life which is promised when we come home to God, through the way of Jesus Christ, then we accept the need to return to the sources to enter into a deep conversation with the Bible and to go through a period of defamiliarizing, of piercing through the obvious in order to enter the real. We trust in the spiritual capacity of people, beloved by God, to detect the still small voice which follows on the great tempest. We trust in the deep things of God and in the weakness and wisdom of God more than we trust in hip-hop makeovers.

We are called not to fidget with our image but to grow into a Christ-like character, something deep and slowly formed by the action of the Spirit of God, through prayer and worship. The Church is concerned with depth not décor.

The future comes into being and the Christ-like character is formed in the world as we contemplate Jesus Christ whose story is told in the scriptures and whose life, as gift and invitation, is held out to us in baptism and communion.

As we gaze upon him 'through whom all things in heaven and earth have been created', through whom it is the Father's pleasure 'to reconcile all things to himself, having made peace through the blood of his cross', God lifts us up together to see all creation, as he intended, brought into joyful symphony.

Sometimes our neighbours are disappointed to find that we have substitutes: in-house preoccupations of our own for this divine vision of reconciliation. We are sometimes clearer what we are against than what we are for. We fuss about churchy things. A handbook on needlework in the 1950s prescribes that 'the length of the lavabo towel should be 12 inches for RCs and 18 inches for Anglicans'. Why Anglicans should be so mucky as to need the larger towel, I know not.

As we gaze upon Christ and his character is formed in us, his future becomes flesh and blood. Christ leads us as his students, his disciples, to enrol others in a future which bears at least these four marks of 'the good pleasure of the Father'.

1. Whole persons are brought home to God through the way of the cross. Cut off from God, human beings fulfil less than their potential. Through prayer and worship and walking the way of the cross, we must play our part in re-telling and enacting the story of what Jesus Christ has done. It will take every ounce of our God-given imagination to

reveal the beauty of the story so ancient but so fresh. Everyone has a role in this work.

2. The Church of Jesus Christ shall be one and whole. It was his will and commandment that we should be one. This is not a matter of tactics but an essential part of the Father's good pleasure and a contribution to achieving his intention that the whole world should dwell in symphony. Be impatient for unity among Christians. Do not retreat into a secretarian mentality. Jesus Christ pleads with us to help build his great and coming Church.

3. There will be one, whole humanity. Joy and fullness of life do not flow from dis-related pleasure-seeking. Individual persons are unique and precious but they grow and flourish only to the extent that they are in communion with other persons. If the Christ character is being formed in us then we shall be partners with people of good will, no matter what their belief or apparent lack of it, to feed the hungry, heal the sick and to build one whole humanity.

When the Christ character was formed in him, St Anthony the Great was able to sum up the Christian life thus, 'My life and death are in my neighbour.' The Catholic movement in the Church of England gained ground finally because of the self-sacrificing love of slum priests like Father Lowder who worked just down the road in the London docks. Christ calls us to contribute to the symphony with one another for everything and to be responsible for one another in everything.

4. Lastly, in the Father's pleasure there will be one whole creation, animate and inanimate, which we

shall all be able to enjoy and see, as God did in the beginning, that it is good and beautiful. The creation faces the threat of a godless project of human exploitation without limits, with no end in view beyond the process itself. We are alive at a time when means pretend to be ends. As we see more and more through the divine love in the face of Jesus Christ 'through whom all things in heaven and earth were made' we shall find ourselves in partnership with all those who are concerned for the health of the planet and who know that in the end there will be one world – or none.

Christ is not only our vision of the future but our way in to it. Only in his strength can we see this challenge and not be daunted by it. Today we celebrate not a demo or a show of party strength or a churchy triumph. We celebrate because he has promised, 'I am with you always even unto the end of the world.'

London Arena
10 June 2000

12

Whitsunday

'We do hear them speaking in our own tongues the
mighty works of God.' So said the great gathering of
believers in Jerusalem from all over the world come to
celebrate the Pentecost, the fiftieth day after the
Passover, when the first-fruits of the corn harvest were
offered in the Temple.

The business of the Christian life is to acquire the
Holy Spirit. This is not done by giving ourselves airs,
putting on a special voice and speaking in an artificial
spiritual manner. Instead, the preparation for the events
described in the Acts of the Apostles was obedience to the
command of Jesus Christ that his followers should 'wait
in the city' until the gift was poured out upon them.

Waiting in the city means laying ourselves open to
receive the gifts of God by attentive and expectant love
and being educated by silence and stillness and by
prayer, which is tuning in to the wavelength of the
Holy Spirit. The icons of the saints are written with
large ears for hearing the communication of God, large
eyes for seeing his works, and very small mouths. The
Church often gets the balance between proclaiming
and listening wrong. I pray for a Church in which

meetings of the Synod are concluded early because the Spirit has not spoken.

I returned last week from a pilgrimage to our partner church in Berlin where there was also a great gathering of Christians from all over the world – 400,000 of them, Catholics and Protestants, Orthodox and even a sprinkling of Anglicans. We worshipped together in the city and reclaimed the streets which had until recently been the theatre for state-sponsored communist demonstrations.

I am a poor linguist and mostly use Europanto which relies on bold gesticulations, but deprived of the possibility of chattering I experienced powerful and refreshing communication in the Spirit. The Spirit opens up a channel of communication heart to heart, subject to subject, and this brings joy. You didn't have to know German to understand what was being communicated.

Much of the evil in the world comes from treating other people as objects. In the wisdom locked up in our language we 'size people up, cut them down to size, overlook them'. Lethal ways of relating to other people as if they were objects instead of temples of the Holy Spirit can damage health and create the conditions for antagonism and lethal conflict.

The world is hungry and thirsty for the gift of the Holy Spirit which brings joy and unity. London and Berlin have been enemies. The Berlin festival was a vision of a whole world reconciled in Christ through the Holy Spirit.

But there was an alternative vision to be seen in the German capital. I visited the new parliament building and marvelled at the technological sophistication of its solar-powered air conditioning. I was then shown the room where Parliamentarians go to meditate. There upon the walls are six large panels. In the first there is a field of earth set with flints. Our guide explained the second panel in which human beings first appear as a clutch of white painted nails. In the third panel the nails are arranged in various religious symbols, cross and crescent. By the fourth panel, the nails dominate the whole surface. In the fifth panel there has obviously been some disaster and the nails are much diminished and in retreat. In the final panel the field of earth and the flints have returned and you can just see traces of the nails within the stones as part of the fossil record.

It is a chilling vision of the end time when the sun shall be turned into darkness, as the prophet says. It is a vision of what will happen if human beings continue to live as if they were unaccountable masters and possessors of the earth and closed to the Holy Spirit who makes us participants in the inexhaustible life which flows from God.

The Holy Spirit unites us with God, the Beyond All, and with the well-spring of divine life which is in the heart of our own beings although covered up by the debris of past failure and disappointment. The business of the Christian life is to acquire the Holy Spirit, so that the Church can overflow with the Spirit for the sake of a hungry and thirsty world. Are we this festival day, together in this place, like the apostles, really ordering our lives so that our growth in the Holy Spirit for the sake of the world is the very centre of our existence?

St Paul's Cathedral
Whitsunday 2002

13

Midnight Mass

The telephone rings. It is Christmas Eve. A Sunday newspaper is doing the usual survey on whether bishops believe in the Virgin birth. 'Bishop, do you believe? Yes or No?' Now this is a very familiar Christmas game. If you say yes, the assumption is that you are a gullible simpleton who believes in fairy stories. If you say no then it is a scandal that you do not believe what you are paid to believe.

It is for this reason that I always decline to take part in such silliness but if *you* asked me, I would say that my answer is, yes, I believe profoundly and that God 'hath at the end of these days spoken unto us in his Word made flesh'.

The truth, which waits to unfold itself more and more in the story of the birth of the Christ child, is more than mere informational truth, which gives us a few additional facts about life in this universe. It is transformational truth. To as many as received the Christ child, says St John, God's way of communicating himself, his Word, 'to them gave he power to become children of God'.

If we approach and receive the story of the birth in

the stable in the right spirit, then we come to the possibility of being grasped by the truth that life at its heart is not cold and pointless, a tale told by an idiot full of sound and fury signifying nothing, but created out of love and promise. Ours is a story of hope and promise, which is haunted by fear and followed quickly by the massacre of the innocents. The great enemies of making spiritual progress are religious and scientific literalism, superficial readings of life which stop at information and avoid the great deeps.

Think of a noble Christmas oratorio, say Handel's *Messiah*, a sublime piece of music; how would you explain what it was? You could describe it in terms of musical notation, the crotchets and quavers on the score. Or you could go into the science of vocal cords, pipes and their dimensions, the wind in the organ, catgut and tension in the string section. All this is of course true, but it is not an exhaustive account of the oratorio.

Soon you get to the point of what the words, 'Unto us a child is born' and the music mean in their depth and dialogue. In the case of great music, no account you can give is entirely exhaustive; there is always much more to be said. So finally one falls silent and all that we have learned is integrated into our listening, the music works upon us and we have made the passage into transformational truth.

Contemplating the birth of Jesus Christ and understanding him afresh in the light of the universe unveiled by Galileo, Darwin and Einstein, brings you through informational truth to transformation. We have fresh understanding of the depth of the darkness in this universe which is indeed in travail, unfinished, in which there is both birth and death, in which the heavens wax old, as does a garment. They shall perish but God continues, and at the heart of the turmoil there is love and there is promise. So when I am asked whether I believe in the Virgin birth, my answer is yes, profoundly, but I recognize that my answer is likely to be misunderstood by people who are only familiar with the literal approach to the Bible and who have perhaps also been exposed to scientific literalism. It is sometimes so exciting to have caught a glimpse of one aspect of the working of the universe that one is tempted to say, 'That is the bottom line, there is no more depth to be discovered.'

Some of the followers of Darwin (though not Darwin himself) have suggested that our moral and religious aspirations are guileful evolutionary contrivances deluding us into the groundless belief that we are cared for by a providential reality. This delusion has been useful, however, as our genes seek a circuitous path to immortality.

This privileging of just one level of explanation, claiming that there is nothing deeper, is like becoming fixated with the science of vocal cords, pipes and their dimensions, and missing the music. In any case, intuitively it does seem implausible that such an easily detectable fraud could have had such positive evolutionary consequences, which presumably now will not follow, as the fraud has been unmasked.

Biblical literalists are in fact in thrall to the way of thinking made popular with the rise of scientific literalism. This is a modern phenomenon not typical of the way in which the Bible was read in the springtime of the Christian movement. When they ask about the

Virgin birth, the big question for them is, 'Did parthenogenesis really occur?' It certainly did in experiments on turkeys in Pennsylvania University. The story of the birth of Jesus Christ is much more than some gynaecological singularity.

Perhaps the visit of the Magi makes it clearer. Here are research scientists, cosmologists in fact, who are dissatisfied with the level of knowledge and information they have attained through long years of observation. They go on a journey, an uncomfortable journey, 'a cold coming we had of it' with political complications following the subject of their own studies, a star in the heavens. But their story is not an allegory whose meaning can be extracted without following the way. The story points us to the way to transformational knowledge, to the birth of the Christ child, not only far away and long ago, but here and now, in St Paul's, in us. But notice: just as scientists have to undergo a long preparation to be able to perceive the truth which lies beyond the obvious, so that is the case with those who would be transformed by the truth. So often he comes unto his own and his own do not receive him because they have not disciplined themselves to see.

The child was born to a young woman who had no conventional hope of such a birth, such a Godsend. But at a time dominated by the iron laws of economics and political calculation she was attentive, she looked for depth and was grasped by the truth that the mercy, the love and the promise, the very Word of the Creator was alive within her and was expressing himself within and through her. That is transformational truth. We pray to God, this Christmas, that he will enable us to contemplate this birth in the way which leads to transformation into the children of God.

St Paul's Cathedral
24 December 2003

Part 3

On Various Occasions

14

John Fisher Commemoration

John Fisher was beheaded on 22 June 1536, for refusing to take the King's oath.

A prayer of John Fisher before a sermon: 'I beseech thee Almighty God . . . that whatever I shall say may first be to thy pleasure for the profit of mine own wretched soul and also to the wholesome comfort to all sinners.'

There could not be a better way of beginning Christian Unity Week than among Christian friends in this liminal place to honour the living memory of a great Christian and a holy Bishop, John Fisher.

It is particularly good to welcome our Cardinal and my brother of Rochester. This is a place of ecumenical adventure, for here I, as Dean, am not responsible to myself as Bishop of London.

Any dialogue between churches involves an early recognition that our traditions involve different views of history, and often the histories imputed to others are not owned by them.

What, you might say, are a brace of Anglican bishops doing, celebrating the life and martyrdom of someone who was judicially murdered by King Henry VIII?

After all, I hear a voice crying out, it was Henry who founded your Church, was it not?

That is not of course the understanding that the Church of England has of itself. Henry was a monster of egoism with a gift for propaganda. As the brilliant edition of some of our most disreputable fantasies and served by some very gifted artists, he has continued to fascinate and even impress posterity as he impressed and terrified his contemporaries. John Fisher had the courage to make clear his judgement on the king's policy and proceedings while he was in the tyrant's power – and he paid for his candour with his life.

All the churches of Europe were reformed in the sixteenth century, and alas, in the process the Western Church was fragmented with consequences that haunt us to this day. It was the great age of the cartographer and the drawers of lines in the sand. Nation states consolidated their boundaries and co-opted religious establishments of all kinds in the process. It was a time when Christians were tempted to over-define mysteries in the interests of polemics. No church emerged from the sixteenth century without radical change for good and for ill.

John Fisher was himself a reformer, a fact which his martyrdom has tended to obscure. He has been miscast as an unbending champion of the old order, but the truth is more complex. In addition to the excellent life by E. E. Reynolds, new light has been shed on Bishop Fisher's theological position in Richard Rex's admirable book.

He was a Cambridge reformer, a reformer of his beloved university and a promoter of the study of Greek and Hebrew which opened the way to a fresh engagement with the word of God in scripture. Fisher himself was a copious preacher at a time when bishops tended to be more involved in juridical and strictly sacramental concerns. He knew very well that the Church needed reform and a renewal of its spiritual life – which of course it always does.

In his controversies with continental Lutherans, Fisher discerned and concentrated on the essential issues. As Rex says, he pushed to one side the debates about the value and application of the merits of the sacrifice of the Mass. Instead, 'taking up patristic and mediaeval parallels between the Real Presence and the Incarnation' as well as drawing on a reading of John 6, he fashioned an incarnational ecclesiology that made the Real Presence 'an indispensable part of the economy of salvation'.

He also opposed the particular course which the Reformation was taking in England, and especially the assumption by the king of the Supreme Headship of the Church. It was Fisher who insisted on the insertion in legislation of the phrase 'as far as the law of Christ allows', but the arbitrary nature of the Caesaro–Papist Supreme Headship was fully asserted by Henry in the Act for the Restraint of Appeals. Fisher's clarity about the vocation of the See of Rome in the service of unity is a challenge and an inspiration as we grapple in our own day with the difficulty of maintaining international unity among Christians.

He spent 14 months imprisoned in a cell which General Field has shown me. Already venerable, his head was struck off on 22 June 1535. We honour his memory close to where he is buried. We honour his protest against any state with Messianic pretensions. His example is still eloquent even though the form in which Henry had asserted his ecclesiastical powers did not of course survive his reign, and they were not revived by Queen Elizabeth.

We salute the courage of Bishop Fisher, but above all the discernment, which came from prayer and study of the scriptures, of the issues which were really at stake in the ebb and flow of political fortune. His devotion to John the Baptist is significant in a life which always penetrated the camouflage to reveal the real issues. Others absorbed in the game, like Stephen Gardiner, could not see where they had become accomplices or where they had failed to say no. This is a lesson for all time.

Bishops Fisher, Latimer, Ridley and Cranmer themselves are united in death as they were tragically divided in life. They are all enrolled among those who, however reluctantly, at the end died for their loyalty to principle and conscience. In this our day, what are we prepared to die for? If we can give an answer to this question then it gives a clue as to who we are. Any church that is too comfortable in the world as it is and has lost the capacity to discern when it ought to be saying 'No', such a church is far away from the gospel which Fisher preached and for which he died.

> The Chapel Royal of St Peter ad Vincula in
> HM Tower of London
> *19 January 2004*

15

The Magi:
Millennium Window

How good to be here to dedicate your splendid new window showing the kings bearing gifts to the Christ child.

You have of course decided to pay tribute to a development of the story we heard from Matthew's Gospel. The Magi have become kings under the influence of certain Old Testament prophecies and, as you know, especially if you have visited Cologne where the kings are truly celebrated, the story has had a long history of elaboration. But even as we have it in Matthew, there are other echoes and influences.

The picture of Magi coming from the East to pay homage to the new king would not have struck Matthew's readers as naively romantic. When Herod the Great completed the building of Caesarea Maritima just before Jesus was born, envoys from many nations came with gifts. Then, not long before the date of the compilation of the Gospel, an event took place which captured the imagination of Rome. In 66 AD, according to Dio Cassius, Suetonius and Pliny, Tiridates King of Armenia, with three young Parthian princes in his train, came from the east and 'paid homage' to Nero.

After Nero had accepted their homage, the sources say that the king 'did not return by the route which he had followed in coming' but sailed back a different way. Pliny describes the delegation as 'Magi'.

What then is the deeper reading of the story of the Magi in Matthew's Gospel? Here are research scientists, cosmologists in fact, who are dissatisfied with the level of knowledge and information they have attained through long years of observation of nature. They go on a journey, an uncomfortable journey, 'A cold coming we had of it' with political complications following the subject of their own studies, a star in the heavens.

St Simons Zelotes
18 January 2004

16

Healthy Living;
Healthy Dying

The Temple of the Divine Healer Aesculapius in Pergamum, in modern-day Turkey, is a ruin now but must
once have been a most salubrious place. The memoirs
of a valetudinarian from the second century AD, one
Aelius Aristides, who enjoyed ill health in this ancient
hospital, give us some notion of what was on offer.

In the Greek medical tradition the fundamental
recipe for healthy living was 'Know thyself and be
moderate in all things' and this outlook was expressed
in the regime followed in the hospital. There was
dream therapy to gain access to the energies of the
irrational. There was even a small theatre where those
in search of healing could write and perform their own
plays. Lying just outside the bustle of the town, the
temple must have been a tranquil and beautiful environment in which to recover in an atmosphere which
was a cross between Champneys and an Oxbridge
college.

The emphasis on moderation in all things was
expressed particularly in the close attention paid to
diet. Surgery was available from those who had gained
experience treating gladiators and so had a good

working knowledge of some of the simpler procedures.

It was in the ruins of this place that I remember contemplating the theme of healthy living and healthy dying. Aelius and his friends were of course from the wealthy leisured class, and there was no sophisticated health care available for most of the population.

And I am no medical Luddite. The progress in medical science in the past hundred years is a proper cause for celebration and thanksgiving. As recently as the mid-nineteenth century, so I read in a book of sovran remedies, the suggested treatment for whooping cough was to drink water out of a bishop's skull – 'when available' says the book. Rather worryingly from my perspective, a suitable skull seems to have been available in County Cavan in the 1830s. When asked whether I should have liked to be alive at any other time than this, I think of dentistry and say no.

But contemplating other visions of what constitutes healthy living and restoration of health can help us to frame some useful questions for our own time.

One of the most obvious things about the Pergamum approach is that it assembled in one place and in one regime a number of elements of a holistic vision of healthy living which are now commonly practised in isolation or whose significance is not noticed at all.

Our knowledge is vast, but partly as a consequence it is fragmented into a number of specialisms held together by a language of management which can only work with what is measurable and quantifiable.

The fragmentation of our knowledge and its consequences for the care we offer is vividly illustrated by Sir Cyril Chantler in a recent article in the *Health Service Journal*. He describes a situation in which a community nurse visited an elderly lady twice a day to administer eye-drops. Carers were visiting her three times a day but were not allowed to administer the drops. One day the nurse forgot the keys to the house and the old lady had a fall on her way to open the door. The police broke down the door but the nurse was not allowed to pick up the old lady so an ambulance was called. The patient protested that she was fine, but she was taken to hospital and then returned home at 11pm after the carers had left. There is nothing in all this but the best intentions, but somewhere the idea of caring for the whole person has become obscured.

Max Weber, in an analysis that is still valuable, talks of the essence of modernity being the 'differentiation of the cultural value spheres'. He was referring to art, morals and science. Most pre-modern cultures did not differentiate these spheres clearly, but modernity differentiated art, morals and science, and let each pursue its own truths in its own way, free from intrusion. This resulted in a spectacular growth of scientific knowledge, a flurry of new approaches to art, and a sustained look at morals in a more naturalistic light.

The distress, however, arising from pursuing these ways of thought in isolation from the other spheres is, however, becoming more evident. There are many examples. One is the autistic way in which we relate to the environment, only feebly aware that we are damaging the web of life in which we are in reality participants, not masters. Another is the way in which we discuss the global economy without relating number-based economic analysis to broader questions of human well-being. The Germans have identified

'Das Adam Smith Problem' which centres on the difficulty of relating some of the doctrines derived from Smith's late work, *The Wealth of Nations*, to the insight he gives into how societies thrive in his earlier book, *The Theory of Moral Sentiments*.

We are nowhere near even the beginning of a new summa, but this is the time for expeditions into neighbouring spheres in an effort to find some unitive and integrative concepts which can signal a way to transcend the present distresses.

In so many areas there is search for a new holism and nowhere more so than in health. One of the ways of describing healthy living is as a continuing and developing personal identity in balance with and actually nourished by gifts and challenges from the environment.

Clearly in this perspective, one of the important tasks facing us is to direct appropriate attention and resources to primary health care and education, especially in the matter of diet where the agenda has so often been hijacked by commercial lobbies. There does seem to be a wide measure of agreement on what constitutes a healthy diet, and it does not depart very greatly from the advice given in the Hippocratic tradition. I have recently found the scientific basis for proverbial wisdom in this area particularly powerfully expressed by Dr Joel Fuhrman in his recently published book *Eat to Live*.

His advice differs very little from the teaching of John Wesley, whom I have been re-reading in his 300th anniversary year. John Wesley wrote a book entitled *Primitive Physic* for his followers in which the virtues of plain food in moderation, labour with eight hours' rest, and the cultivation of a calm and contented spirit are celebrated.

Sometimes, however, the system breaks down and we need help. We are fortunate in having so many possibilities, but in the accumulation of new knowledge it is possible to overlook the obvious. The healing environment itself needs to be therapeutic since a calm and contented spirit is clearly conducive to recovery of healthy living. It is difficult to quantify such effects however, and in consequence there is a danger that this dimension of healing becomes invisible.

The Western churches have a confession to make here: they have played a part in casting into shadow the social and the relational aspects of healthy living and healthy dying by sometimes narrowing their discussion of what constitutes salvation to focus on mental assents and dispositions. The word used in the New Testament for 'salvation' and the verb 'to save' both include the idea of the restoration of physical well-being and healing, and do not simply point to some supposed spiritual part of ourselves. Salvation in the Christian tradition was originally a holistic notion which was bound up with building a health-giving community.

If the language we use implies that health is a commodity which can be acquired by individuals as a result of greater investment, or even bought or sold, and if the whole debate is dominated by commercial interests, then vitally important aspects of healthy living are edited out of the picture.

Another consequence is that the health of poor people receives insufficient attention world wide in a way that would be intolerable if it were happening in our own country. I have been fascinated by the visibility of the SARS epidemic despite the mercifully small numbers involved so far in Western cities. The subject is an important and serious one and should have been given publicity, but there is a sobering contrast with the relative invisibility of the carnage inflicted on the children of Africa by malaria. According to a Tanzanian researcher, the death toll is equivalent to seven Boeing 747s crashing into Mount Kilimanjaro every single day.

African culture has other lessons to teach us. In Alison Webster's excellent book *Well Being* she tells the story of learning an African language in which the common form of greeting is 'How are you?', to which the standard reply is, 'I am well if you are well.'

Healthy living as distinct from sanitized living depends on a web of connectedness and nourishing relationships. Part of our social distemper is that this condition for healthy living is not taken sufficiently seriously in our policy-making and institution-building. Healthy living demands a right relationship with the world within and nourishing relationships with others. That is of course not all.

Despite the valuable lessons of Darwin who reconnected us with nature as creatures of the earth like Adam (whose name in Hebrew means creature of the dust), our capacity to live in touch with nature and our own flesh, both developing and respecting it, has been undermined by the extent to which we live in our heads and fantasies. We need to refresh our awareness of the web of life in which we are participants.

There is another dimension without which the optimum conditions for healthy living cannot be fulfilled, and that is some connection with the Beyond All and some sense of meaning in life. The project in which so many of us seem to be entoiled, that of growth without limit with no end in view beyond the process itself, is not, I believe, conducive to healthy living.

The time when many of these relationships come most sharply into focus is when we face death. It is sometimes considered morbid to contemplate one's own death. John Donne the poet and Dean of St Paul's had himself painted in his own winding sheet as a way of facing his own mortality. The marble representation of that painting was one of the few things to survive from Old St Paul's to be incorporated into Wren's building.

Our failure to face our own fear of death is an important reason why we find it so difficult to help the dying and the bereaved. One of the most common things you are told by dying persons is that they feel that they are somehow in the way. The bereaved say that their comforters are too quick to try to distract them from talking about the spouse or the friend who has died. We try to gloss over the fact of death by using euphemisms, and we are protecting ourselves very often when we exclude children from funeral services or even the sight of dead bodies.

Our hectic style of life owes much to the suppressed fear of death and the unexamined notion that the faster we live, the more we shall get out of this short life.

Hospices are places where we can experience and experiment with a different way of healthy living and healthy dying. The marvellous discoveries about pain control are an essential part of the service, but medical intervention is subservient to exploring the potential in dying for health – health defined as the sustaining and development of a personal identity nourished by the resources and challenges of the environment and, most importantly, our multi-dimensional relationships. A hospice is a window onto another vision of healthy living and healthy dying, and on countless visits to different hospices I am nearly always struck by how transforming the experience is for those involved, and how few complaints there are. They are not on the whole gloomy places; instead they can induce a sharper appetite for life nourished by the spectacle of persons who, while being physically diminished, are at the same time being spiritually enlarged.

Hospice care is of course expensive because it is staff-intensive. An overemphasis on the valuable tools of target setting and measurement could easily obscure the importance of what is being achieved, not only for those who are dying but for the health of everyone involved.

The myth of Prometheus to whom modern man has frequently been likened is very instructive. Prometheus literally means the fore-thinker, the rational planner. He is a heroic figure, but the bird representing his mental processes is at work in the daylight world, gnawing at his vitals and the seat of his emotional and imaginative life. Only by night do these vital organs grow back, and we find it very difficult to do justice in the daylight world when we consider healing to give proper value to these dimensions of the one human reality.

I refuse to be cynical and hopeless however. There is a growing appreciation that approaching health as a commodity governed by the same rules that apply to the supply and sale of all commodities edits out essential parts of the picture. It is one interesting sign that as religious practice in the community at large has declined, so the number of chaplains appointed by NHS trusts has substantially increased.

If we wish to build healing environments to help people with the business of healthy living and healthy dying, then as well as injecting funds we need stability and a truce to constant re-organization which tends to undervalue the time needed to develop trusting and effective therapeutic teams. We also need to appreciate and encourage our health professionals more and discourage any further development of the culture of blame.

We also need to strengthen and support institutions like the King's Fund which have the independence and the imagination to campaign for the common good, free from the distortions inseparable from over-dependence on the commercial sector and for a more holistic vision of health for all.

The King's Fund Lecture
20 June 2003

17

The London Centre for Spirituality

St Ignatius of Antioch said that a bishop never more resembles Jesus Christ than when he has his mouth shut. It is an important word of advice on a day like this when there is always the temptation for the bishop to add to the number of monologues stressing the importance of dialogue and discoursing at length about the virtues of silence in our devotional life.

But we meet on the festival day of a more encouraging saint and bishop, a true spiritual athlete, who blesses our gathering. Launcelot Andrewes was a London man through and through, but universal in his spiritual sympathies, as his book *Private Devotions* makes clear. He was at one time a canon in this cathedral and a great scholar, but he was always utterly clear that our persuasiveness as a church is in proportion to our spiritual credibility.

Let the preacher labour to be heard intelligently, willingly, obediently. And let him not doubt that he will accomplish this rather by the piety of his prayers than by the eloquence of his speech. By praying for himself and those whom he is to

address let him be their beadsman before he
becomes their teacher.

The great challenge to the Church of England, as to all
churches, is to be spiritually credible and to speak the
word of God as if it were a transforming event and not
simply a description of what it is. It is impossible to
convey spiritual electricity by reading from the wiring
diagram, no matter how accurately presented. Christian life without prayer is a theory, not a lived reality.

Transformation, however, is costly and involves consistent practice and an ordered life. One cannot toy
with spirituality as if it were some desirable commodity. That is why the method and the accent of the
Centre is and will be on practice, and the cry *'rumpite
libros nec corda rumpuntur'* shall be heard: 'Discard
the books before they clog up the heart' might be a
demotic translation. If we have really set out on some
particular way on the road to everywhere, we know
that the way is hard, and we shall need humour and
humility about ourselves if we are to make progress.
But at least we know that there is no progress to be
made if we simply fancy the idea of being more spiritual and do not commit ourselves to some definite
pattern no matter how crude and provisional. The
Centre should help us all to get in touch with a fruitful
way for our own temperament.

But why do we need a Centre for Spirituality? Is not
every church a centre for spirituality? What's the big
idea?

The Centre is a crossroads for many different
approaches. One of the hopeful signs of our own times is
the spirit of adventure. All over the Church and beyond,

people are looking hopefully at other traditions. The Centre is and will be a place of respectful encounter, as the participation in tonight's service demonstrates.

Someone put into my hands recently a book by Richard Foster. His title, *Streams of Living Water*, is from John 7.38: 'He that believeth on me, out of his belly shall flow rivers of living water.' The semitic belly stands for the spiritual heart.

Richard Foster is from the Evangelical tradition, but in his book you can find a wonderful re-appropriation of rich Christian memory and experience of the kind we are engaged in this evening. Foster, an American, is the founder of Renovaré, a movement committed to spiritual renewal. I will end by quoting Foster's introduction to his book since, as you know, high-flown rhetoric is not really in my line.

Today a mighty river is bursting forth . . . It is a deep river of divine intimacy, a powerful river of holy living, a dancing river of jubilation in the Spirit, a broad river of unconditional love for all peoples. The astonishing new reality is this mighty flow brings together streams of life that have been isolated from one another for a very long time . . . I have tried to name these great traditions.

This night we pray that the new Centre may play its part also in naming these great traditions. May the blessing of God the Holy Trinity and the example of Lancelot Andrewes give his energies to our work. Amen.

St Paul's Cathedral
25 November 2003

18

Encountering God Today

Today if ye will hear his voice harden not your
hearts, as in the provocation and as in the day of
temptation in the wilderness. (Psalm 95.7–8)

Love expresses itself in many ways, in our Diocesan
Housing Association and the campaign for affordable
housing; in the work for rough sleepers at St Martin's
in the Fields Church, London; in the day-in, day-out
pastoral care offered by our parish churches. We need
good organization, clear objectives and efficient finan-
cial management. There is no holiness in a shambles.
But if Christ's healing spirit is to dwell in our pro-
grammes, if we are to communicate the love of God and
his healing attention and not scorch people with our
own hectic condescension, then the work of prayer is
utterly fundamental to everything we seek to do. Apart
from him, cut off from the vine, we can indeed do nothing that will touch the deep inner pain and loneliness,
the alienation, the sense of our being strangers to our
own good which afflicts the modern city.

But we pray not only to empower our work but
because in prayer we find in God our true selves. We

hand over our egoism and he waters our soul and gives us a foretaste of life with him in eternity.

I have been asked to reflect on some aspects of this situation under the heading 'Spirituality and Religion'.

There is a perfectly proper use of the word 'spirituality' when it qualifies some tradition of faith. There is clearly such a thing as Christian spirituality and Sufi spirituality. I imagine, however, that the organizers wanted me to reflect on the naked spirituality, which is immensely popular in influential circles, not least in education: a spirituality which is contrasted and sometimes opposed to traditional religion.

There are many good things about the revival of interest in spirituality, and it is for the Church to reclaim ground which it ought never to have lost, by appearing to so many people spiritually incredible.

The increasing concern over the past two decades about the spiritual development of young people in our schools represents a welcome shift of emphasis from an undue preoccupation with the content of what is to be taught to a consideration of how the awareness of the learner might be deepened and enlarged.

The yearning for an understanding of spirituality which would contribute to social cohesion has led to the establishment of a new orthodoxy in which it is suggested that access to a realm of universal spiritual experience can be achieved by primal intuitions unconstrained by any particular religious tradition. In this new orthodoxy, Christianity and Islam are represented as, at best, local and partial editions of this universal spirituality. Mike Newby, writing as an expert in religious education from Kingston University, puts the matter very clearly:

For reasons of tact and discretion, it is unwise to specify offending sub-traditions, as well as politically and socially harmful. It is important however if we are to develop an integrative system of values that we give up pretending to show respect for authorities that inhibit change by repressing unrestrained enquiry.

This new orthodoxy is presented as universal in its scope, but it may prove to be a rather short-lived provincial fashion confined to this phase of Western culture. It plays well of course in a phase of culture which regards the world as just a theatre for unrestricted human willing.

The hollowness of the new orthodoxy will become evident the more people realize that we have surreptitiously deified our personal tastes in place of the dialogue with the divine which informs the traditions of the religions that revere Abraham.

In any case, the primal spiritual intuitions that are supposed to exist find little recognition in the reductionist views of human beings that are increasingly taking hold. The rhetoric of human dignity, shorn of the Christian context, which gave rise to this way of regarding human beings, begins to look desperately implausible. We begin to suspect that we might be in fact little more than rapacious bipeds whose happiness consists in consuming the world and one another.

It is certain that the new orthodoxy can only become a new establishment by radically distorting the Christian spiritual tradition. The accent in so much modern discussion of spirituality is on the passage from dependence to independence in which the person is freed from various constraints in order to be able to construct a reality founded on personal preferences. The tradition of Christian Trinitarian spirituality also involves a passage from dependence and the domination of fears and cravings to independence and freedom. But this passage is undertaken as a preparation for committed interdependence. In the Christian tradition, freedom is for relationship and encountering God, and transcends freedom from constraint.

I was sitting next to someone at a City gathering the other night and they turned to me with that elaborate politeness which expresses the condescension of a superior being so far removed from the vulgar prejudices of a mere bishop. The question was, what exactly was Christian orthodoxy when Christian ways of prayer and organizing the Church and dressing priests seemed to be so different? From some place the answer came to me. The crucial frontier is between those who believe that there is a set of universal spiritual truisms to which we can have access, entertain as our ideas, and to which the life of Jesus, in part at least, points. They stand on one side of the line. They are in the Church of Nicodemus who arrived at Jesus's door in the night of unawareness in John 3 and who immediately tried to fit the Lord into his own mental categories. Jesus does not comment but invites him to be born again, and the 'Teacher of Israel', as Nicodemus is called, is baffled. On the other side of the line is the Church of the Samaritan serial divorcee in chapter 4 of John's Gospel. Christian orthodoxy is immensely varied, as we can see from today's workshops, but the crucial affirmation is that God has communicated what otherwise we could never have known. He has communicated in the person, the life, death and resurrection of his Son Jesus Christ. The beginning of true religion is annunciation, a communication from the side of the other to Abraham, Samuel, David, Mary.

If we do not believe this, or at least admit the possibility that it might be true; if the Church accepts the dominant mode of reasoning in our late Western culture, then in the words of the Canadian Anglican writer George Grant, prayer, worship, all the ingredients of 'public religion becomes an unimportant litany of objectified self-righteousness necessary for the more anal of our managers'.

But the times are hopeful and today's exercises are a sign of this hope.

Andrew Walker, the Ecumenical Canon of St Paul's, has been talking about the reality of the experience of deep church which lies beyond the polemics of high church, low church and broad church. The phrase 'deep church' comes from C. S. Lewis who used it in a book with a title borrowed from the great Puritan divine Richard Baxter, *Mere Christianity*.

The deep church rests upon two historical givens. One I have already mentioned, God's communication of himself in the person of his Son – revelation. The other is the institution by his Son of the Church, now tragically fragmented by human sin.

The historical memory of what God has done needs to be continually re-appropriated by Christians, and much of what we are doing today is part of that re-appropriation. We need to know what the Church has learned by experience, where and when it took a wrong turn, and what victories it has achieved. There is an amnesia about this record, and if we are to be a deep church there must be an anamnesia. Too many Christians are imprisoned in the present moment with a nodding acquaintance of the New Testament moment which we are therefore almost certain to subject to our provincial views in the here and now. The word of God is set free to speak when we take counsel with Christians of other times and places in our preparation for what Jesus commanded: 'Hear O Israel.'

We need to retell and re-appropriate our story to recover our identity as the people of God. Yet this can be mere gossip from the muniment room unless we experience the presence of God existentially. Here I want to pay tribute to the role played by the Charismatic Revival in the Church in opening the way for us to be a deep church.

Andrew Walker says that 'Church communities that have accessed the living memory without sharing in the life of the Triune God are mere antiquarians.' It is possible, however, to attempt to live in the presence of the Spirit without re-appropriating the Christian tradition, and the experience of our community is that this is the way to fantasy and delusion. To be a deep church, it is necessary, in the words of Baron von Hügel, to respect the intellectual, the institutional and the mystical aspects of life in the Church.

Carpenters' Hall
17 May 2003

19

Celebrating Life

We come together to celebrate life. Obvious you might say – who wouldn't on a day and in a place like this? But actually, to be a real celebrant of life requires a way of being aware in the world which is in harmony with our deepest nature but which can come to seem like a foreign country.

To be a celebrant of life is to be 'aware' in a very special way, and we are in our own days in a time of flattened and diminished awareness. What do I mean?

Our generation is characterized by behaviour which seems to suggest some kind of autism in respect of the cosmos; a certain lack of awareness or recognition which causes us to waste the beauty of the world and to treat human beings not as ends in themselves but as subordinate to the laws of economics.

We have grown into a way of seeing and consuming the world which has made humankind, in the words of the French philosopher Descartes, 'Master and possessor of the earth'. In the world view of such a being, what is seen is not so much an animated nature in which human beings are participants but simply matter to be exploited. Dominance has been substituted for connectedness.

We treat planet earth and one another in a destructive God-forsaken way because we see things in a destructive, God-forsaken way. We see things that way because we have turned our terrible avid gaze, which sees only things and objects to be exploited, upon ourselves. Our form of awareness turns all that surrounds us and our very selves into things. We have become estranged from ourselves.

Behind the rhetoric of humanism, there is a modern self-image of ourselves as rapacious bipeds, little more than utensils for conveying genetic information from generation to generation. The intrinsic sacredness and holiness of human life becomes difficult to perceive, and happiness is seen to depend on things that are added to our lives, things which add up to 'quality of life'.

Fortunately it seems to me that modern science has already provided us with a number of concepts which make the recovery of an authentically Christian and biblical awareness more of a possibility.

Darwinism, whatever its other reductionist tendencies, has returned human beings to their organic place in nature. This has restored the perspective which informs the symbolism of Genesis 2 in which God forms 'Adam', the earth creature, out of the very dust – 'ha'adam'.

The creation which we celebrate continues as we stand here as God ceaselessly breathes the Spirit into his creation. Everything that is, exists and lives in the unceasing inflow of the energies and potentialities of the Spirit. As the psalmist says:

When thou hidest thy face they are troubled:
when thou takest away their breath they die, and
are turned again to their dust.
When thou lettest thy breath go forth, they shall
be made: and thou shalt renew the face of the
earth. (Psalm 104.29–30)

The Spirit is poured out on everything that exists, the
Spirit preserves, makes it live and renews it. If the
Holy Spirit is poured out on the whole creation then
she creates the community of all created things with
God and with each other. 'In him we live and move and
have our being' (Acts 17.28).

As the prophet William Blake claims:

Everything that lives,
Lives not alone, nor for itself.

A Christian awareness will see the world, neighbours
and indeed ourselves as imbued with the Spirit which
makes them 'good and beautiful'. When God contemplates his work in the creation narrative and sees that
it is 'good', the Hebrew word implies goodness and
beauty.

Manichees hate matter. Pagans worship matter.
Materialists are (ironically) indifferent to matter.
Christians give thanks and refer matter to the Creator. If we wish to be celebrants of life, the prayer
of thanksgiving is indispensable: grace before food
unapologetically, and indeed grace before all the other
common marvels of daily life.

Such prayer plays a part in elevating the whole
cosmos to the point where God's intention is realized

and all is bound together in Christ. Part of being converted is turning from being solely a consumer to being a good citizen, a contributor and a contemplative.

One of the ways in which many of you are celebrating life is in resisting the propaganda which often comes from well-intentioned people but which suggests that human life without certain attributes is of no value.

I feel very strongly about this because my only brother, who died in his twenties from cancer many years ago, but still has a great influence on me, was so mentally handicapped that he could never lead an independent life. I suppose if medical science had been more advanced in those post-war years he might well have been a candidate for termination. His love and the 'Yes' he gave to what would seem to some as a very restricted form of life transformed the relationships and the attitudes of those who knew him. I am a priest because of his witness.

I find the same incredible 'Yes' to life in a letter which was published in the *Daily Telegraph* newspaper at the end of last year. The correspondent suffers so many afflictions that she says that many would consider her 'better off dead', and indeed she had herself believed this for many years; if euthanasia had been legal she says she would have requested it. Then she writes, 'I am alive now only because my friends refused to go along with my view that my life had no value. Over time they enabled me to re-establish a sense of my own inherent dignity and worth.'

This is of course no argument for over-treatment of patients of the kind that a recent survey by the *American Journal of Medicine* said was prevalent in that country in a system driven by the insurance industry and the fear of litigation. I welcome the BMA guidelines to which considerable publicity has been given this past week, but I believe that all the decisions we make in this complex territory should be informed by an awareness of the 'inherent dignity and worth' of human life. This is an awareness which only comes with celebration of life and resistance to all the forces which suggest, sometimes in compassionate tones, that life is only worthwhile if we are in full possession of our faculties.

Hatfield House
4 May 2002

20

Invitation to Prayer

St Paul prays that Christians may be strengthened
with might by the Spirit of Christ in the inner person.

We have responded to an 'Invitation to Pray' for peace
and justice in the world at a time of great international
turmoil. There are certain views of what we have been
urged to do which are not credible. The bombardment
theory is one such sub-Christian view. The idea that
prayer is stirring God up to do what otherwise he would
not have done is rooted in misunderstood picture
language about God.

The reality is that God is closer to us than our conscious mind knows. There is a deep structure to the
world and also to the human person (St Paul calls this
realm the inner man) which is obscure to us as we are
caught up in the hectic business of the passing
moment. Imagine a game of chess. On the surface it is
all motion, with pawns being scythed down, knights
galloping about the place and of course bishops always
approaching things slant-wise. But beneath this surface play there is the deep structure of the rules of the
game and the board itself. A crust forms which keeps
us locked in the passing moment, unaware of the deep

structure where God expresses his almighty love and justice in what you might call the Maker's Instructions.

The invitation to prayer is an invitation to pierce that crust by calling out in words but then in silence and stillness in order to enter into that deep inner world which is called, in scripture, the spiritual heart – that Christ may dwell in our hearts by faith.

Prayer is not preaching ourselves a sermon about noble concepts like peace and justice; it is piercing the crust of unawareness so that the energy of God can do his work in the daylight world.

Especially at a time of crisis we need to root and ground ourselves in the love that we see in Jesus Christ, the human face of God, so that we do not get carried away by gusts of indignation which come from our fear.

We pray for God's peaceable wisdom in ourselves, and because all creation is interconnected we pray especially for our brothers and sisters who are facing hard decisions about how to defeat apocalyptic terrorists who believe that they are religious, have not made any specific demands about feeding the hungry or justice in world affairs, but are bent on destroying the whole international order. At such a time we need the clarity, the wisdom and the courage that comes with deep and simple prayer.

Buckingham Palace Chapel
5 October 2001

21

With All Thy Heart and With All Thy Soul

Now Israel, what doth the LORD thy God require
of thee, but to fear the LORD thy God, to walk in
all his ways, and to love him, and to serve the
LORD thy God with all thy heart and with all thy
soul. (Deuteronomy 10.12)

Israel – us, called to this place on this morning full of
doubt or anger, just hanging on to our faith, or joyful
and convinced; mysteriously God has called us and the
Holy Spirit is at work within us.

What is the first requirement for progress from
wherever we start? Fear? All very well for those with
the experience of oriental despots: but we have a
constitutional monarchy. We do not like to talk now of
fearing God, and suspect something nasty in the
Freudian woodshed and think of abusive parents.

It is true that the world is full of the grandeur of
God, and awe is appropriate; but 'Fear the Lord thy
God' in this context means more like the words in that
Scottish motto: 'Gang warily.' People are tempted to
reduce God to a moon, when he is a sun and source of
life; to make him into an asset when he is the subject of

the whole drama of creation in which we are involved. The true journey of faith begins when we wake up, when we become aware of the reality of God, that all things point to him as the needle points to magnetic north. As soon as we have this inkling, when we 'arise, take our journey' if we ever have, we go warily because a landscape is disclosed in which God and his messengers are everywhere.

Fear involves being aware. That happens first by the grace of God, but this awareness is deepened with spiritual practice, by silence and stillness – the great educators.

In the silence and the stillness of daily meditation where we, with great simplicity, wait upon God, the shadows in our inner life gradually come into focus. It is important to be relaxed and unafraid as we see through these shadows. Our attention and waiting on God is so different from the state which is induced when some overbearing teacher barks the command 'Pay attention' – the result of that is contracted muscles, and actually less goes in than before. 'Gently does it' when we first become more attentive to the Spirit speaking within.

But further progress depends on real change where it is necessary. We need detox and decompression continually. If we are to love God with all our heart and soul then our walk must be transformed. We cannot love God whom we have not seen if we do not love our brothers and sisters whom we have seen. Journeying into God demands generous living. Don't cheat, don't lie, don't defame, but do give in generous measure.

If we are not truly humble and down to earth then it is possible that we may soar into mystical flights with a God with whom we can identify, but we shall be flirting with a projection of ourselves and come crashing down to earth like a second Icarus when we approach the real sun in all his glory.

The journey to loving God with all our heart and soul, the living and true God who is not the product of our fantasies, is pursued by a growth in awareness, by a growth in a holy life, a life of integrity. But if we wish to be a person who passes over into the promised land: who comes to participate, as St Peter says, in the divine nature and not just talk about it, then the prayer of longing love must be our way.

Here is a great divide in the road. It is possible to treat God as if he were a commodity: 'You have tried drugs and sex now try God for the ultimate high.' This is an ancient way, and in plainer days it was called magic, which is all about getting and imposing our will and agenda. The way of the Christian mystic is quite different. Magic is about getting; mystical prayer, the prayer of longing love, is about giving, which is why generous living is a preparation for contemplating God. The fourteenth-century mystic, John Ruysbroeck, said 'When love has carried us above all things . . . we receive in peace the Incomprehensible Light, enfolding us and penetrating us . . . We behold that which we are, and we are that which we behold; because our being without losing anything of our own personality, is united with the divine truth.'

In the orgy of retrospect which still brings the events of the Second World War to our screens every week, I am not surprised that one sixtieth anniversary in the past week has passed without any mention. Sixty years ago last Friday, in the Trinity season of 1941, Evelyn

Underhill passed to her rest. Her many books and writings on this journey into the promised land can still be read with profit. For those with a strong constitution, her book on mysticism is a masterwork. For Moses, the pilgrimage leading to the promised land began with a bush which flamed with a fire that burned but did not consume – a precise description of the experience of the longing love of God. Evelyn Underhill wrote with a similar inside understanding of the journey into the burning bush, although she lived in prosaic circumstances in Campden Hill Square with a husband who was a bluff fellow who did not go in for that sort of thing. She was a person of humour and was delighted to find in a florist's tulip list a bulb called 'The Bishop. A bloom of great substance. Blue base with white halo, borne on a stiff and upright stem.' She was loyal to the Church of England, though often exasperated by it – in short, she was one of us.

Nevertheless she remains one of the greatest modern guides to the journey into the promised land which involves the effort and the suffering of conversion. Conversion means making progress in the way of life which leads us from our common starting point as consumers of life through the stage of being good and contributing citizens of a commonwealth to the point where we are contemplatives of the God of infinite possibility. Consumers, citizens, contemplatives – that is the map of the way into the promised land. The Lord said unto Moses, 'Arise, take thy journey, go in and possess the land.'

Chapel Royal, London
17 June 2001

22

My House is a
House of Prayer

How good to be in this holy place again, more than 35 years after I sat here in the pew as an undergraduate and saw just a little beyond the horizon of my understanding.

In the seventeenth century, after being the Chapel of Peterhouse for many years, Little St Mary's Church in Cambridge reverted to being a parish church just in time to be visited by William Dowsing, who among other things destroyed 'God the Father sitting in chayer and holding a Glasse in his hand'.

Most of what we can see is the result of the nineteenth-century restoration which followed a period in which contemporaries doubted whether any human hand could save the Church of England.

We do not for the moment face plague or iconoclasm but there is undoubtedly confusion about the identity of our Church, mutterings about a death by dignity, doubts about whether we are entertaining or relevant enough. The acid is working away at all institutions. Much that is beautiful and venerable seems to be under threat. Critics and the scoffers sometimes seem to be the really effective evangelists, converting us into people who look for someone else to blame or else tempting us to more and more hectic salesmanship.

And yet, if we have learned anything from worship in the cool passion of the catholic tradition in the Church of England, it is that God has 'such a quiet manner of existence that those who name him with a loud insistence show that they've forgotten his proximity' (Rilke, Rainer Maria, *The Book of Hours*, Book I, §64, trans. J. B. Leishman). Such times send us back with sharper ears and more open eyes to the scriptures. I want to address the Gospel story of the merchants in the Temple.

We could get into the historical and cultural background and talk about the Temple tax that had to be paid in a particular coin, Tyrian shekels – hence the money-changers. This is not, however, a story about the evil of cathedral shops but something deeper.

Jesus entered the Temple of God and drove out all who bought and sold. In one of his greatest sermons, commenting on this text the German medieval mystic, Meister Eckhart, said, 'The merchants must go when truth is revealed; for truth needs no merchandising.'

This church is intended to be the gateway to the Temple of the living God. As we enter, we immerse ourselves with great simplicity in the Spirit-filled tradition, the continuous stream through time which wells up in holy scripture and which opens the way, as St Peter says, for us to become 'partakers of the divine nature'. There is all the difference in the world between immersion in this tradition and traditionalism which is the obstinate defence of a cultural artefact, a commodity. The Church is not an institution which caters for people's religious tastes and feelings, whether high-brow or demotic, but it should be an entry into the Temple of the living God where there can be no negotiation but rather there must be simplicity and vulnerability.

Everything flows from our growth in praying with simple awareness. This church has been, as it is now, a place where this prayer is practised and deepened.

Communication with the true and living God comes to those who are profoundly aware, often whose awareness has been heightened by some challenge, some joy or suffering, confirmed by sober, persevering prayer.

If we wish to hear the still, small voice in our own lives more and more clearly, then meditating day and night is part of the preparation which builds the house of true prayer and lays the foundation for our assembly on this, the eighth day of new creation. Taking the time to be still and silent. In great simplicity, respecting the body, keeping our back straight and using some simple prayer because 'out of the mouth of babes and sucklings thou hast brought perfect praise'. This is a prayer nourished by hearing and digesting the Bible so that we can come to hear the word addressed to us in the inner spaces.

Richard Crashaw, who knew this church just before it was vandalized, clearly knew the way

    Discourses dy!
Keep close, my soul's inquiring ey!
Nor touch nor tast must look for more
But each sitt still in his own Dore.

This simple prayer is frustrated if, instead of desiring to draw closer to God who said, 'I am with you', we treat him as an object of our thought and even a commodity to be merchandized.

Marx was not wrong about everything and he prophesied that the nemesis of this civilization would be that everything and everyone would be turned into a commodity. Even God has had his merchants in recent times – 'you have tried other stimulants, they fail in the end, try God'. If God is an object of our thought then we are in touch with a thought projection of ourselves – the channels between our spiritual centre and the true and living God are not open. The merchandizing has to stop and the attachments severed.

As we grow in this kind of prayer, if we do become uncluttered, quiet and attentive – aware of how we speak, of our motivations, of how we try to evade the morning and evening meditation – then we shall see very clearly some of the shadows that are within us all, our refusal at some levels to love and be loved.

Do you see that it is no accident that after the expulsion of the merchandizers 'the blind and the lame came to him in the Temple and he healed them'. He could heal those whose disability was obvious to themselves, but the merchants of God, those who came with commodities and concepts, were filled with indignation. Jesus Christ helps us to see the shadows within and to see through them in a way that drains them of power.

If we shy away and cover up with things – our office (chief priests and scribes), status or success, academic or otherwise, instead of becoming more and more aware – then the shadows will grow in power like some swelling within and will make themselves felt in all kinds of ways.

What we cover up, we give it power to harm; what we see in our daily prayer, Jesus Christ can heal. Those who know their need for forgiveness and that they are forgiven are those who can speak with convincing authority even in days when voices of authority are treated with suspicion. Solomon's prayer shows this ancient wisdom: 'Hear thou in heaven thy dwelling place and when thou hearest forgive.'

The present vicar recalls meeting Archbishop Runcie coming out of Little St Mary's. He said, 'I save up my prayers for my visits to Little St Mary's.' This has been a place, despite plague and iconoclasm, where prayer has been valid, a real door into the worship of what St Augustine recognized as 'thou Beauty both so ancient and so fresh . . . and behold thou wert in me and I out of myself where I made search for thee'.

Little St Mary's Church, Cambridge
3 November 2002

23

Robert Runcie

The last occasion on which I heard Robert Runcie speak in public was in support for another abbey, St Albans. There had been some muddle about who was to speak, and Robert modestly suggested that he was a mere substitute, and he told a story about Bishop Donald Coggan. Archbishop Coggan had been invited to a garden party with the promise of a strawberry and cream tea. When approaching the gate, however, in common with the other guests, he was handed a note which read, 'Owing to the unseasonable unavailability of strawberries, prunes will be served.'

That's how I feel now. Robert Runcie was himself the master of the memorial address and I suspect that only he could have done justice to such a rich life.

Typically, however, he was modestly dubious about this occasion and wondered whether it would be really necessary. In the event, the Abbey has not been able to hold the number of people who have applied for tickets. The diversity of those of us who have assembled this morning testifies to Robert Runcie's gift for friendship and the breadth of his sympathies and interests. We profess or are agnostic about many faiths. We come from many countries, from every part of the Christian Church, and from the provinces of the Anglican Communion. Yet we come not as formal representatives but drawn by a sense of personal friendship for a man who was and is greatly beloved.

I can see him in my mind's eye now, a relaxed style of delivery giving no hint of the meticulous preparation and hard work which went into his public addresses. He had a great respect for the Word and a good ear for which words were still potent and usable and which had become decrepit. He also had a penetrating intellect and could spot the flaws in arguments so readily that it made the process of composing public statements very laborious; but his gifts were perhaps most obvious in the thousands of personal letters of sympathy and encouragement which he wrote in his own hand.

This was hidden work, and there was much about his deepest convictions which was also hidden. As with so many of his generation, wartime service was formative. He did not often refer to those years, but the death of a comrade, and the revelations at Belsen of the dark side of human nature played a large part in pushing him towards ordination as a priest. Firsthand experience of the horror of the Shoah also gave him a lifelong commitment to Christian–Jewish relations. He was part of a generation of priests marked by the war who believed that the Christian community still had the potential to change the world.

In the years following, he worked hard, in Gosforth, back in Cambridge and at Cuddesdon, anxious not to let people down. At the same time, he also had a pronounced competitive streak which came out in his convictions for speeding on the Stevenage bypass while he was Bishop of St Albans. He made the sports pages of the *Daily Mirror* and he became the hero of the churchwardens of the Diocese.

The role of Archbishop of Canterbury is very frequently frustrating. The Archbishop is mistakenly compared by the world to a managing director and blamed for every conceivable failure in the Church, but when he attempts to bring about some change and seize the levers he finds that there are no connecting rods. Archbishops lead by setting a style which can be deeply influential but which often does not translate easily into a list of achievements.

This is a generation of seekers, who are sceptical of ecclesiastical claims to have all the answers and who demand seriousness about the mystery and the paradoxes of life and suffering. As we heard from Robert Runcie's enthronement sermon, it was his talent and ambition to communicate with such people.

The 'Soul of Britain' survey which was commissioned by the BBC records the familiar fact that the credibility of all institutions, including the churches, continues to decline. At the same time, however, the numbers of people admitting to significant personal spiritual experiences have greatly increased over the past decade. Under half the sample answering similar questions, in 1989, could point to significant experiences of the spiritual realm. By 2000, this figure was over three-quarters of those questioned. One of the most frequent tributes to Robert as a Bishop is that whatever the doubts and questions of the person he was with, he was able to meet them where they were without judging them or preaching at them.

He was a very contemporary Christian leader in another respect. The Church of England had a central part in the nineteenth-century version of *Our Island Story*. The end of the Empire, a more cosmopolitan British population, and our participation in a wired-up world presents a challenge to the nature of British identity and also to the identity of the Church of England. Robert made a contribution to developing a new identity in a process which has perhaps only just begun. He was a wonderful ambassador and has made connections which bore rich fruit.

The equation of Catholic and alien was part of the old story. The way in which the Pope was received at Canterbury in 1982 was an important milestone in honouring the Roman Catholic strand in our history. Robert had first met the Pope in Africa at the start of his Archiepiscopate. The encounter was to take place in Accra, Ghana. Robert briefed Cardinal Hume by telephone about what was planned. The Cardinal was enthusiastic but finally asked, 'But Robert, there's one thing I do not understand: why is it necessary to meet the Pope in a car?'

The Canterbury service was the very first time in the history of the West that the Pope had participated in the worship of a non-Roman Catholic Church, and *pace* certain commentators, John Paul II certainly behaved as if he were visiting a sister Church. Pope and Archbishop stood side by side before Augustine's chair, where a book of the Gospels was enthroned: the very book sent by Pope Gregory the Great to the first Archbishop of Canterbury.

A little later, in connection with the 500th anniversary of the birth of Martin Luther, Robert as

Archbishop visited Germany, and the work he did was a major stimulus for the Meissen Conversations and Agreement which followed. The former Bishop of Berlin is present with us today.

Through a demanding programme of visits to the churches of the Anglican Communion, he encouraged Anglicans towards a new inclusive and confident identity by personal friendship and by telling the story of the connection in a way that defused any suspicion of English condescension.

His stamina was remarkable. After a month in Nigeria, in the hottest time of the year just before the rains, his aides, Terry Waite and the Chaplain, were exhausted; but the Archbishop was still valiantly working through his programme. We reached Kano and the Archbishop of Nigeria indicated a TV camera and said to Cantuar, 'Pray for the rain.' He did so. That afternoon the heavens opened and our Muslim driver said, 'You'll be remembered in Kano.'

Making new connections and embracing a more cosmopolitan identity was work which continued to the very end of Robert's earthly life. A fortnight ago the *Oxford Companion to Christian Thought* was published, edited by the distinguished scholar Adrian Hastings. It contains an article by Robert Runcie on Canterbury. Typically the author admits that the city is 'a comparatively modest urban centre in Kent' but he goes on to place Canterbury in a more cosmopolitan history with mentions of previous Greek and Italian archbishops, the architecture of the French Gothic and French Protestant congregation which has worshipped in the crypt since the sixteenth century. In the article, as throughout his ministry, he remembers in a way that established a new inclusive identity and reaffirms Canterbury's place in the effort to heal the 'historic divisions of Christianity'.

He has been accused of being too inclusive and emollient, and in a famous phrase, of firmly nailing his colours to the fence. Refusal to get down into the trenches can give the community a chance to live through difficulties without being atomized.

But where a firm stand was necessary, the Archbishop spoke out for Christian conscience. In the Falklands Service at St Paul's his note was Christian and penitent rather than triumphalist, as some desired. He was also attacked for his role in the publication of the *Faith in the City* report on deprivation in inner-city areas. What was rubbished then as 'Marxist' is now accepted wisdom. But typically the report was not just a demand that the government or someone else should do something, it was a challenge to the Church. The report led to the establishment of the Church Urban Fund, which is still doing creative work in the inner cities. It also changed lives. One priest said to me, 'It gave me a new sense of pride in being part of the Church of England.'

St Augustine of Hippo in his pithy way described the Christian community at its best '*In certis, unitas. In dubiis, libertas. Et in omnibus caritas.*' 'In the fundamentals of faith there must be unity. In disputable matters there must be freedom for debate. But in everything there must be love.'

Robert's convictions formed and tested in struggle were deep, though hidden behind a veil of reticence. In worship these deep springs were refreshed. It is particularly appropriate that the choir will very soon sing the Creed from the Russian Orthodox tradition which appealed to Robert so much. There were bedrock certainties that gave him the strength not merely to tolerate but encourage different opinions among those with whom he chose to work.

'*In certis, unitas. In dubiis.*' But the most lasting thing is love. Family life was not without its occasional tempests, but family was the place where Robert could be entirely himself. Lindy, James and Rebecca, and now a wider family, were and are united in love. Robert was a man greatly beloved by a huge circle of friends.

In the latter years, after Robert had laid down the burden of office, this element of his life was distilled out. Many people, once they have lost the trappings of status and visible power, shrink. Robert, by contrast, seemed to shake off a role that had become constricting. He became more himself. The playfulness of earlier years revived. His sympathies continued to enlarge. He made no secret of his cancer, but far from becoming self-obsessed, there are people here who can testify that his ability to encourage others who were locked in the same battle, increased.

We believe that what has turned to love in our lives will never perish. St Paul said that, though our outward man perish, yet the inward man is renewed day by day (2 Corinthians 4.16).

We miss him, his friendship and his humour, but in the midst of the tears we can, in the word which rings through the first lesson, rejoice.

Westminster Abbey
8 November 2000